Celebrating GREAT COOKING with Pastene

BRIMAR

Chef and food stylist: Josée Robitaille
Photography: Nathalie Dumouchel
Graphic design: Zapp

Props courtesy of: Stokes, Ramacieri Design, Pier 1 Imports

Front cover photograph: Vegetarian Salad with Black Olives,
page 78; Sicilian Bruschetta, page 10; Chicken Breasts with
Capers and Sundried Tomatoes, page 150, served with
pesto fettucine; Fresh Asparagus with Vinaigrette, page 48.

Back cover photographs: Four Bean Salad, page 85;
Barbecued Pork Chops with Artichokes, page 146;
Bocconcini Pizza with Pesto, page 46.

Published by Brimar Publishing Inc.
338 Saint Antoine Street East
Montreal (Quebec) Canada H2Y 1A3
Tel. (514) 954-1441 Fax (514) 954-5086

Canada
The publisher thanks Heritage Canada
for the support awarded under the Book Publishing
Industry Development Program.

Printed in Canada

Contents

Pastene Pas

"America's First Taste of Italy"

When Luigi Pastene arrived in Boston in 1848, he earned a living by selling fruit from a pushcart in the Italian section of the city. By 1870, he had built his tiny business into a recognized fruit and produce company, employing his son Pietro as clerk and bookkeeper. In 1874, Pietro took over the management of the company and consolidated its operations as an import house.

At the time, Boston was entering a period that would see its harbor flourish with shipping traffic for decades. Wooden ships, then steamships arrived and departed daily, carrying cargoes from Africa, Asia, and Europe; their safe arrival at the mercy of chance, skill, and the elements. American trade was expanding, and while the American frontier was growing and General Custer was preparing for what would be his last stand, the business of the times was still largely controlled by the port cities of Boston and New York.

In 1907, the Pastene Company opened offices in New York and Naples; in 1911, Montreal followed. In 1912, the company established branches in Rome and Havana, and opened the Pastene olive oil packing plant in Imperia, Italy.

The first 40 years of Pastene was a time of steady growth and dynamism blueprinted by Pietro Pastene and executed by his son, Charles A. Pastene. Peter A.

Pastene, another son, ran the daily operations of the company. On the death of Charles Pastene, the company was passed to his cousins, the Tosi family. Charles Tosi established a dynamic policy of streamlining which kept the company flexible and viable during difficult years.

In 1999, as Pastene celebrates its 125th anniversary, its leadership remains progressive and dynamic, earning the company a commendable reputation for its choice imported Italian tomatoes, delicate olive oils, fine Italian vinegars and a variety of other imported foods. In addition, Pastene offers a line of domestic food products, from canned vegetables to breadcrumbs, and continues to develop innovative, quality food products for the USA and Canada.

We at Pastene are proud of our Italian heritage and of our tradition of quality products. Our commitment to quality will remain a priority as we expand into the next millennium.

Celebrating Great Cooking with PASTENE

The secret to good cooking starts with high quality products, and the secret to Pastene quality starts with our own special sources and blends. Here are just a few of our favorites.

TOMATOES

Tomatoes, as we all know, are an essential component of many Italian dishes. Healthwise, tomatoes are low in fat and calories, and they are rich in antioxidant properties, making them an essential component for a healthy diet. Pastene carries a full range of canned tomato products to suit every recipe and cooking style. Our select sundried tomatoes, dried naturally under the hot Italian sun, are available in bulk or packed in oil.

OLIVE OIL

All Pastene olive oils are extracted from olives in three steps: the olives are crushed; the oil and water from the olives are separated; then impurities are filtered out. **Pastene Extra Virgin Olive Oil** is produced from the first cold pressing of olives. Its flavor is characteristically green and fruity. **Pastene Pure Olive Oil** is a blend of olive oils, combined and refined to balance the acidity, aroma and taste. **Pastene Extra Light Olive Oil** is filtered to produce a paler color and less pronounced flavor, with no loss of nutritional value. It is useful for baking and frying, because it can be

heated to a higher temperature. Olive oil is higher in healthy monounsaturated fats than any other oil on the market, and there is plenty of scientific evidence demonstrating its health benefits. So for flavor, nutrition, and versatility, olive oil is the obvious choice.

WINE VINEGARS

Pastene Wine Vinegar has complex wine flavors, which result from a blend of different varieties of grapes. It's perfect when you want to spice up a salad, create a zesty marinade or add flavor to sauces. Balsamic vinegar originated in the northern Italian town of Modena. **Pastene Balsamic Vinegar** is darkly rich and syrupy, with intense, complex flavors. It is the result of a careful fermentation based on the must of sweet grapes, then aged in oak barrels for a minimum of four years before bottling.

BRUSCHETTA

The charm of **Pastene Bruschetta Tomato Topping** is its ease and simplicity. It is a delightful combination of diced tomatoes, oils, herbs and garlic, made from a recipe passed down for generations, and ready to serve on lightly toasted crusty bread, as a pizza topping, or as part of an antipasto platter.

Arborio Rice is the critical ingredient in the famous risotto dishes that originated in the north of Italy, and which are now popular everywhere. Quality **Pastene Arborio Rice** is the perfect choice for turning out a successful risotto.

Anchovies add a distinctive flavor to a wide range of Italian specialties. **Pastene Anchovy Fillets** are canned in pure olive oil.

Capers are the unopened flower buds of the caper shrub, which grows in the Mediterranean region. **Pastene Capers** are marinated in vinegar, and add a piquant flavor to a variety of salads, sauces and main dishes.

Crostini
and
Bruschetta

Take a few slices of toasted crusty
bread, drizzle with luscious extra
virgin olive oil, and top with simple,
flavor-packed mixtures.
Nothing could be easier!

The savory morsels called *crostini*,
originally created to use up stale bread,
have become the classic Italian-style
starter. Heartier *bruschetta* started out as
the working man's snack food, but with
the addition of today's inventive
toppings, they can be served as an
appetizer, a snack or even a light meal.

Whether you're in the mood for finger
food or something more substantial,
you can count on Pastene's fine
products to provide you with an
unlimited choice of memorable flavors.

SEAFOOD
Bruschetta

makes 6 pieces

18	medium shrimps	18
½ lb	bay scallops	250 g
4 tbsp	PASTENE Extra Virgin Olive Oil	60 mL
3 tbsp	fresh lemon juice	45 mL
1 tbsp	grated lemon zest	15 mL
2 tbsp	fresh parsley, chopped	30 mL
1	small garlic clove, minced	1
1	bay leaf	1
6	slices of crusty Italian bread	6
1	jar (8½ fl. oz/265 mL) PASTENE Italian Bruschetta	1
	PASTENE Extra Virgin Olive Oil for drizzling	
	salt and freshly ground pepper	

• Devein shrimps by making a shallow cut along outer curve and washing away any black vein under running water. Peel off and discard shells.

• Cook shrimps in boiling salted water for about 5 minutes. Lift from water and let cool.

• Meanwhile, cook scallops in same boiling water about 2 minutes. As soon as scallops are opaque, drain into a colander. Let cool.

• Combine shrimps and scallops. Add olive oil, lemon juice and zest, parsley, garlic, and bay leaf. Season to taste with salt and pepper. Stir gently. Let marinate about 1 hour at room temperature or up to 24 hours refrigerated.

• If refrigerated, let warm to room temperature before continuing. Remove bay leaf from mixture.

• Grill bread until golden and drizzle with olive oil. Top with Bruschetta and shrimp mixture. Serve immediately.

SICILIAN
Bruschetta

makes 8 pieces

8	slices of crusty Italian bread (½ in./1 cm thick)	8
¼ lb	smoked Mozzarella, shredded	100 g
1	jar (8½ fl. oz/265 mL) PASTENE Italian Bruschetta	1
	PASTENE Extra Virgin Olive Oil for drizzling	

- Toast bread until barely golden. Drizzle lightly with olive oil. Sprinkle cheese evenly over bread slices, leaving a border (about ¼ in./.5 cm) all around.

- Place bread slices under a preheated broiler for a few seconds, or until the cheese bubbles.

- Drain the Bruschetta and spoon over the melted cheese. Serve immediately.

PROVOLONE AND MUSHROOM
Crostini

makes 24 pieces

2 tbsp	**PASTENE Extra Virgin Olive Oil**	30 mL
12	fresh mushroom caps, quartered (or a 15-oz can **PASTENE Straw Mushrooms, drained)**	12
1	garlic clove, crushed and chopped	1
1 tbsp	fresh parsley, chopped	15 mL
1 tsp	fresh oregano, chopped	5 mL
24	slices of French bread (baguette), oiled and toasted	24
4 tbsp	**PASTENE Black Olive Paste**	60 mL
4 oz	Provolone cheese, sliced	100 g
	parsley and oregano for garnish	
	salt and pepper	

- Heat oil in saucepan over high heat. Add mushrooms and garlic and cook 5 minutes, stirring occasionally.
- Season to taste with salt and pepper. Add parsley and oregano. Set aside.
- Spread toast with olive paste. Top with mushroom mixture, cheese and herbs.
- Broil under preheated broiler until cheese melts. Serve immediately.

CROSTINI
with Sundried Tomatoes

makes 30 pieces

1	jar (9 fl. oz/280 mL) PASTENE Sundried Tomatoes in Oil, well drained	1
2 tbsp	fresh basil, chopped	30 mL
1 tbsp	fresh oregano, chopped	15 mL
1 tbsp	PASTENE Extra Virgin Olive Oil	15 mL
30	slices of French bread (baguette), lightly toasted	30
⅔ cup	PASTENE Grated Parmesan Cheese	150 mL
	freshly ground pepper	

- Preheat broiler.
- In a bowl, mix tomatoes, basil, oregano and oil. Add pepper to taste.
- Spread on toasted bread and top with Parmesan.
- Broil until golden and serve at once.

TOMATO AND ROMANO
Crostini

makes about 36 pieces

1	can (28 fl. oz/796 mL) PASTENE Italian Peeled Tomatoes, well drained	1
1 tbsp	PASTENE Tomato Paste	15 mL
5	garlic cloves, crushed	5
1	green pepper, chopped	1
½ tsp	Tabasco sauce	2 mL
1 lb	PASTENE Grated Romano Cheese	500 g
	French bread (baguette), sliced, oiled and toasted	
	salt and pepper	

- In a saucepan, cook drained tomatoes, tomato paste, garlic, green pepper and Tabasco over medium heat, stirring occasionally, until thick.
- Stir in grated cheese until melted. Season to taste with salt and pepper.
- Serve hot on toasted bread slices.

CHICKEN AND ANCHOVY
Bruschetta

makes 8 pieces

2	**boneless chicken breast halves**	2
3 tbsp	**PASTENE Pesto Basil Sauce**	45 mL
½ tsp	**pepper**	2 mL
4 tbsp	**PASTENE Pure Olive Oil**	60 mL
8	**slices of crusty Italian bread, brushed with oil and toasted**	8
2 tbsp	**PASTENE Grated Romano Cheese**	30 mL
4	**PASTENE Anchovy Fillets in Oil, drained and halved**	4
½ cup	**PASTENE Italian Bruschetta, drained**	125 mL

- Brush chicken with pesto. Let marinate 1 hour. Season with pepper.
- Heat oil in medium skillet. Add chicken and cook over medium heat 8 minutes on each side, or until no longer pink inside. Remove from skillet and let stand 5 minutes. Slice chicken.
- Arrange chicken slices on oiled toast. Top with Romano, anchovies and Bruschetta. Place on broiler tray under preheated broiler for 2 minutes, or until cheese is lightly melted.

GRILLED SHRIMP
Crostini

makes 12 pieces

6	slices of crusty Italian bread	6
1 tbsp	PASTENE Balsamic Vinegar	5 mL
¼ cup	PASTENE Extra Virgin Olive Oil	60 mL
1 tbsp	fresh tarragon, chopped	15 mL
1	garlic clove, minced	1
12	large raw shrimps, shelled and deveined	12
4	PASTENE Roasted Peppers, cubed	4
	PASTENE Extra Virgin Olive Oil for brushing	
	fresh tarragon for garnish	
	freshly ground pepper	

- Cut each bread slice in half diagonally. Brush with oil and toast lightly. Reserve.
- In a bowl, combine vinegar, oil, tarragon, garlic and pepper to taste. Toss shrimps in mixture until well coated. Cover bowl and let marinate in refrigerator 30 minutes.
- Remove shrimps from marinade and grill over medium heat for 6 minutes on each side, or until tender, brushing with marinade occasionally.
- Arrange pepper cubes on toast. Top with shrimps and garnish with tarragon.

ASPARAGUS
Bruschetta

makes 4 serves

16	asparagus spears	16
1 tbsp	PASTENE Pure Olive Oil	15 mL
1 tsp	PASTENE Balsamic Vinegar	5 mL
8	slices of crusty Italian bread, toasted	8
1	jar (8½ fl. oz/265 mL) PASTENE Italian Bruschetta, drained	1
¼ cup	PASTENE Grated Parmesan Cheese	60 mL
	salt and pepper	

- Preheat oven to 400°F (200°C).
- Snap tough ends off asparagus and discard. Peel and wash spears, pat dry and place in a baking dish. Pour olive oil and vinegar over asparagus and roll spears until evenly coated. Season with salt and pepper to taste.
- Cover dish with foil and bake 10 minutes or until asparagus is tender.
- Top toasted bread with Bruschetta and 2 asparagus stalks, cut in 2. Sprinkle Parmesan over top. Serve immediately.

Snap tough ends off asparagus and discard.

Peel and wash spears, pat dry and place in a baking dish.

Pour olive oil and vinegar over asparagus and roll until evenly coated. Season with salt and pepper. Cover dish and bake until tender.

Top toasted bread with Bruschetta.

Top Bruschetta with 2 asparagus stalks, cut lengthwise in 2.

Sprinkle shaved or grated Parmesan over top. Serve immediately.

BRUSCHETTA
with Bocconcini and Basil

makes 12 pieces

4	balls of Bocconcini cheese,* drained	4
12	thin slices of crusty Italian bread	12
1	jar (8½ fl. oz/265 mL) PASTENE Italian Bruschetta	1
8	fresh basil leaves, chopped	8
	PASTENE Extra Virgin Olive Oil	
	dried oregano	

- Preheat oven to 450°F (220°C).
- Cut Bocconcini into 12 slices. Drain well on folded paper towels (otherwise Bruschetta will be soggy).
- Arrange bread rounds on a baking sheet. Brush each lightly with olive oil.
- Place a slice of cheese on each bread slice. Top with Bruschetta. Sprinkle with basil and oregano and drizzle with a few drops of olive oil.
- Bake for 10 minutes or until cheese melts. Serve immediately.

Small balls of fresh Mozzarella.

OLIVE AND SUNDRIED TOMATO
Crostini

makes 24 pieces

2	**PASTENE Roasted Peppers**	2
16 oz	cream cheese, at room temperature	500 g
⅔ cup	**PASTENE Sundried Tomatoes in Oil, chopped**	150 mL
¼ cup	**PASTENE Pitted Olives, sliced**	60 mL
1 tbsp	fresh thyme, chopped	15 mL
24	slices of French bread (baguette), oiled and toasted	24

- Chop peppers and mix with remaining ingredients until smooth.
- Spread on toasted bread and serve immediately.
- You can also use this mixture as a dip for raw vegetables.

BRUSCHETTA
with Olives and Capers

makes 8 pieces

1	can (14 fl. oz/398 mL) PASTENE Pitted Olives, sliced	1
2 tbsp	PASTENE Capers in Vinegar, drained and finely chopped	30 mL
1	garlic clove, minced	1
½ cup	PASTENE Extra Virgin Olive Oil	125 mL
8	slices of Italian bread	8
1	jar (8½ fl. oz/265 mL) PASTENE Italian Bruschetta	1
	fresh oregano for garnish	
	salt and pepper	

- Combine olives, capers, garlic and half of the olive oil. Season to taste.
- Brush bread slices with remaining oil. Place under preheated broiler until golden.
- Spread toasted bread with Bruschetta, then olive mixture. Serve immediately, garnished with fresh oregano.

CROSTINI
with Black Olives

Makes about 24 pieces

1 cup	PASTENE Pitted Black Olives	250 mL
3	PASTENE Anchovy Fillets in Oil, drained	3
3 tbsp	PASTENE Capers in Vinegar, drained	45 mL
3 tbsp	PASTENE Extra Virgin Olive Oil	45 mL
3 tbsp	fresh lemon juice	45 mL
1	French bread (baguette), sliced (½ in./1 cm thick)	1
	freshly ground pepper	

- In a blender, mix olives, anchovies, capers, olive oil and lemon juice until mixture is creamy.
- Serve on slices of toasted bread, sprinkled with pepper to taste.

SARDINE
Canapés

makes 12 pieces

Mayonnaise

2	egg yolks	2
1 tbsp	strong Dijon mustard	15 mL
1 tbsp	PASTENE Garlic Vinegar	15 mL
1 cup	PASTENE Pure Olive Oil	250 mL
1 tbsp	lemon juice	15 mL
	salt and pepper	
6	slices of crusty Italian bread, toasted	6
3	cans (4 oz/125 mL ea.) PASTENE Sardines in Oil, well drained	3
	fresh parsley and olive slices	

- To make mayonnaise: In warm dry bowl, whisk together egg yolks, mustard and vinegar until pale in color; season to taste with salt and pepper. Add oil drop by drop, whisking constantly. Whisk in lemon juice.

- Cut toast slices in pieces about the size of a sardine. Spread each piece with mayonnaise and top with a sardine.

- Garnish with parsley, olives and a dab of mayonnaise and serve immediately.

CHEESE BRUSCHETTA
with Dried Tomatoes

4 servings

1 cup	Marsala wine	250 mL
12	PASTENE Dried Tomatoes	12
¼ cup	PASTENE Grated Romano Cheese	60 mL
¼ cup	PASTENE Grated Parmesan Cheese	60 mL
½ cup	Provolone cheese, grated	125 mL
¾ cup	fresh basil, finely chopped	175 mL
¼ cup	fresh thyme, finely chopped	60 mL
½ cup	PASTENE Extra Virgin Olive Oil	125 mL
1	garlic clove, minced	1
8	slices of crusty Italian bread	8
1	jar (8½ fl. oz/265 mL) PASTENE Italian Bruschetta	1

- In saucepan, bring wine and tomatoes to a boil. Remove from heat and set aside for 25 minutes. Drain tomatoes, and set aside.
- Preheat oven broiler.
- Mix cheeses and herbs; set aside.
- Combine olive oil and garlic.
- Brush bread with garlic mixture. Top each piece with some of the Bruschetta, some cheese mixture and a piece of tomato.
- Broil until cheese melts and bread is crisp. Serve immediately.

PANCETTA AND FRESH HERB
Crostini

makes 24 pieces

8	slices of pancetta (Italian bacon), diced	8
24	slices of French bread (baguette)	24
1	garlic clove, halved	1
½ cup	PASTENE Pure Olive Oil	125 mL
2 tbsp	fresh parsley, chopped	30 mL
1 tbsp	fresh chives, chopped	15 mL
⅓ cup	PASTENE Grated Romano Cheese	75 mL

- Preheat oven to 350°F (180°C).
- In a skillet, cook pancetta until crisp and reserve.
- Cut bread in slices (½ in./1 cm thick) and arrange on a baking sheet. Rub each slice with garlic.
- Mix olive oil with herbs. Spread oil mixture on bread slices. Top with pancetta and Romano cheese.
- Bake 7 to 10 minutes and serve hot.

WATERCRESS AND SUNDRIED TOMATO
Crostini

makes 12 pieces

½ cup	PASTENE Sundried Tomatoes in Oil	125 mL
2 tsp	PASTENE Pure Olive Oil	10 mL
1	bunch of watercress, washed and chopped	1
12	slices of French bread (baguette)	12
⅓ cup	PASTENE Grated Parmesan Cheese	75 mL

- Drain tomatoes well, reserving oil. Cut tomatoes in half.
- Heat olive oil in skillet over medium-high heat. Add chopped watercress. Cook about 4 minutes. Drain and reserve.
- Brush bread with reserved oil from tomatoes. Toast lightly.
- Arrange tomato pieces on toast slices. Top with cooled watercress and grated cheese.
- Broil bread under preheated broiler 1 minute, or until cheese is melted. Serve immediately.

Appetizers

A first course before the main meal
is a wonderful way to make family and
friends feel special. Somehow it signals
that what they are sitting down to
is more than just a meal.

Foods chosen as appetizers are
generally light, but filled with flavor.
And because they are meant to prime
the tastebuds for the rest of the meal,
attractive presentation is important.

But that doesn't mean appetizers
must be complicated and take time
to prepare. As you'll see in this
chapter, a few handy Pastene products
can turn even the simplest ingredients
into a gourmet delight!

ROASTED EGGPLANT AND RED PEPPER
Antipasto

4 servings

Vinaigrette

¼ cup	PASTENE Pure Olive Oil	60 mL
2	garlic cloves, finely chopped	2
1 tbsp	fresh basil, chopped	15 mL
1 tbsp	fresh parsley, chopped	15 mL
1 tbsp	PASTENE Balsamic Vinegar	15 mL
4	baby eggplants, sliced (½ in./1 cm thick)	4
2 tbsp	PASTENE Pure Olive Oil	30 mL
1 cup	PASTENE Roasted Peppers, cut in strips	250 mL
	salt and pepper	

- Preheat oven to broil.
- Combine vinaigrette ingredients and set aside.
- Brush eggplant slices on both sides with olive oil. Arrange on broiler pan, in batches if necessary. Broil, turning once, about 8 minutes or until tender.
- Place eggplant slices in a bowl with the vinaigrette. Add salt and pepper to taste.
- Let marinate 30 minutes. Arrange on platter with red pepper strips in center. Serve immediately.

SHRIMPS
Pastene Style

4 servings

1 tbsp	PASTENE Extra Light Olive Oil	15 mL
16	medium shrimps, peeled	16
1	small zucchini, diced	1
2	celery stalks, finely diced	2
2 tbsp	PASTENE Pesto Basil Sauce	30 mL
2 tsp	PASTENE Capers in Vinegar, chopped	10 mL
1 tbsp	PASTENE Wine Vinegar	15 mL
	fresh chervil (optional)	
	salt and pepper	

- Heat olive oil in skillet over high heat. Stir-fry shrimps 3 minutes; set aside.

- Add vegetables to skillet; season to taste with salt and pepper. Cook 4-5 minutes. Stir in pesto, capers and wine vinegar, and set aside.

- Serve shrimps topped with pesto vegetables. Garnish with fresh chervil, if desired.

Heat olive oil in skillet over high heat. Stir-fry shrimps 3 minutes; set aside.

Add vegetables to skillet; season to taste with salt and pepper. Cook 4-5 minutes.

Stir in pesto, capers and wine vinegar, and set aside. Serve shrimps topped with pesto vegetables.

YELLOW PEPPERS
with Parmesan Stuffing

4 servings

2	large yellow peppers	2
1 tbsp	PASTENE Pure Olive Oil	15 mL
1	medium onion, finely chopped	1
1	garlic clove, chopped	1
1 cup	cooked PASTENE Italian Arborio Rice	250 mL
1	can (14 fl. oz/398 mL) PASTENE Italian Peeled Tomatoes, drained and chopped	1
1 cup	PASTENE "Kitchen Ready" Ground Tomatoes	250 mL
2 tbsp	parsley, freshly chopped	30 mL
1 cup	PASTENE Grated Parmesan Cheese	250 mL
	salt and pepper	

- Preheat oven to 375°F (190°C).
- Cut peppers in half lengthwise. Remove seeds and white membranes. Blanch peppers in boiling water 4 minutes. Cool under cold running water and drain well.
- Heat oil in skillet over medium heat. Cook onion and garlic 3 minutes. Stir in rice, season with salt and pepper, and cook 3 minutes.
- Stir in Italian and ground tomatoes, parsley and half the cheese. Cook 7 minutes over high heat. Fill peppers with mixture and top with remaining cheese. Bake 20 minutes.

ARTICHOKE-MUSHROOM
Appetizer

4 servings

3 tbsp	PASTENE Pure Olive Oil	45 mL
½ lb	fresh mushrooms, cleaned and quartered (or 15-oz can PASTENE Straw Mushrooms, drained)	250 g
2	dry shallots, chopped	2
1	garlic clove, chopped	1
1	can (14 fl. oz/398 mL) PASTENE Artichoke Hearts, drained and quartered	1
2 tbsp	fresh parsley, chopped	30 mL
	juice of ¼ lemon	
2 tbsp	PASTENE Grated Parmesan Cheese	30 mL
	salt and pepper	

- Heat oil in skillet over medium heat. Add mushrooms, shallots and garlic; season well. Cook 4 minutes over high heat.
- Add artichokes and parsley; cook 3 minutes over low heat. Sprinkle in lemon juice and cheese. Mix and serve hot, decorated with Parmesan.

SCALLOP AND ROASTED PEPPER
Kebabs

makes 12 kebabs

12	small bamboo skewers	12
2 tbsp	PASTENE Extra Virgin Olive Oil	30 mL
9	fresh mushrooms caps, quartered	9
½ lb	sea scallops	250 g
1	jar (5 oz/170 mL) PASTENE Roasted Peppers, cubed	1
½ cup	PASTENE Flavored Bread Crumbs	125 mL
	juice of 1½ lemons	
	PASTENE Extra Virgin Olive Oil	
	lemon wedges	

- Soak skewers in water 10 minutes. Preheat oven broiler.
- Heat olive oil in a skillet over medium heat and cook mushrooms about 4 minutes.
- Thread scallops, mushrooms and pepper cubes on skewers. Brush with lemon juice and olive oil and sprinkle with bread crumbs.
- Place on broiler pan and place at 2 inches (5 cm) from hot broiler element. Broil about 4 minutes, turning after 2 minutes. Serve with lemon wedges.

FRIED CHEESE
Sandwiches

4 servings

8	large thin slices of Italian bread	8
1 cup	PASTENE Grated Romano Cheese	250 mL
1 cup	PASTENE Grated Parmesan Cheese	250 mL
3	eggs	3
3 tbsp	35% cream	45 mL
¼ cup	PASTENE Pure Olive Oil	60 mL
	fresh chives, chopped	
	salt and pepper	

- Trim crusts from bread. Brush edges lightly with cold water.
- Divide cheeses over 4 slices of bread. Top with remaining slices, pressing edges to seal.
- Place sandwiches on cookie sheet, and place a second cookie sheet on top. Weight with heavy object, such as a large can, for 15 minutes. Cut each sandwich in 4 pieces.
- Beat eggs lightly, season to taste with salt and pepper, and stir in cream. Dip sandwiches in egg mixture. Heat oil in skillet. Cook 4 minutes each side in hot oil. Top with chives and serve immediately.

BASIL CHICKEN
Bites

makes 24 pieces

½ lb	boneless chicken breasts, finely chopped	250 g
¼ cup	PASTENE Plain Bread Crumbs	60 mL
1	egg, beaten	1
1	garlic clove, minced	1
¼ cup	onion, finely chopped	60 mL
¼ cup	PASTENE Grated Parmesan Cheese	60 mL
1 tbsp	PASTENE Pesto Basil Sauce	15 mL
½ cup	all-purpose flour	125 mL
2	eggs, slightly beaten	2
¾ cup	PASTENE Flavored Bread Crumbs	175 mL
2 tsp	PASTENE Extra Virgin Olive Oil	10 mL
	salt and pepper	

- In a bowl, mix chicken, Plain Bread Crumbs, egg, garlic, onion, cheese and pesto. Season to taste with salt and pepper. Refrigerate mixture 15 minutes.
- Shape chicken mixture into small balls. Coat in flour, dip in beaten eggs and roll in Flavored Bread Crumbs. Refrigerate ½ hour.
- Heat oil in skillet over high heat. Cook chicken balls until browned, then reduce heat and continue cooking until no trace of pink remains inside. Serve hot.

TUNA AND CHEESE
Crêpes

4 servings

1	can (6 oz/198 g) PASTENE Light Meat Tuna (Tonno), drained	1
3 tbsp	PASTENE Pure Olive Oil	45 mL
1	red onion, finely chopped	1
3	PASTENE Anchovy Fillets in Olive Oil, chopped	3
½	green bell pepper, diced	1/2
1 tbsp	PASTENE Capers in Vinegar, chopped	15 mL
½ cup	Ricotta cheese	125 mL
2 tbsp	PASTENE Grated Romano Cheese	30 mL
2 tbsp	PASTENE Grated Parmesan Cheese	30 mL
4	prepared crêpes	4
	PASTENE Italian Bruschetta	
	salt and freshly ground pepper	

- Preheat oven to 325°F (170°C).
- Mix all ingredients until well blended. Season with salt and pepper to taste.
- Divide mixture evenly along one side of each crepe. Roll crepe to enclose filling. Place in baking pan and bake 7-8 minutes or until filling is hot. Serve with Bruschetta.

TOMATO
Frittata

4 servings

8	asparagus stalks, trimmed	8
7	eggs	7
¼ cup	1% milk	60 mL
1 cup	PASTENE Grated Parmesan Cheese	250 mL
1	can (14 fl. oz/398 mL) PASTENE Italian Peeled Tomatoes, drained and chopped	1
	PASTENE Grated Parmesan Cheese	
	salt and pepper	

- Cook asparagus in boiling salted water until tender. Drain and chop.
- Beat eggs together with milk and grated cheese. Season with salt and pepper.
- Heat oil in 9-inch (22 cm) ovenproof skillet over medium-high heat. Toss asparagus in oil for 2 minutes. Add tomatoes and cook 5 minutes.
- Add egg mixture and cook about 12 minutes. Meanwhile, preheat broiler. Place frittata in skillet under broiler until top is golden and eggs are just set. Serve topped with shaved or grated Parmesan.

Cook asparagus in boiling salted water until tender. Drain and chop.

Beat eggs together with milk.

Add grated cheese, and season with salt and pepper.

Heat oil in 9-inch (22 cm) ovenproof skillet over medium-high heat. Toss asparagus in oil for 2 minutes.

Add tomatoes and cook 5 minutes.

Add egg mixture and cook about 12 minutes. Then place skillet under preheated broiler until top of frittata is golden and eggs are just set.

BLACK OLIVE AND CHEESE
Dip

⅔ cup	low-fat cottage cheese	150 mL
1 tbsp	PASTENE Wine Vinegar	15 mL
¼ cup	PASTENE Extra Virgin Olive Oil	60 mL
1 tsp	grated orange rind	5 mL
¼ cup	PASTENE Pitted Black Olives (or green olives), chopped	60 mL
1	garlic clove, minced	1
1	green onion, chopped	1
¼ tsp	black pepper	1 mL

• In a blender, combine all ingredients until well blended.

• Use as a dip for vegetables such as carrots, celery, green onions, cauliflower and broccoli, or with crackers, Italian bread or pita bread.

CORIANDER CHICKEN
Kebabs

makes 12 kebabs

2	skinless, boneless chicken breasts	2
4 tbsp	PASTENE Pure Olive Oil	60 mL
2 tbsp	PASTENE Balsamic Vinegar	30 mL
1	garlic clove, minced	1
¼ tsp	black pepper	1 mL
¼ cup	fresh coriander, chopped	60 mL
2	PASTENE Anchovy Fillets in Oil, chopped	2
12	small bamboo skewers	12
	paprika (optional)	

- Cut chicken in bite-size cubes.
- In a bowl, combine olive oil, balsamic vinegar, garlic, pepper, coriander and anchovies. Let marinate 25 minutes.
- Preheat oven to 350°F (180°C). Soak skewers 10 minutes in warm water.
- Drain chicken and thread on skewers. Place on baking pan and bake 12-15 minutes, or until browned. Serve sprinkled with paprika, if desired.

BLACK OLIVES AND SUNDRIED TOMATO
Polenta

(makes 30 pieces)

4 cups	chicken stock	1 liter
1 tsp	salt	5 mL
1 cup	cornmeal	250 mL
1 cup	Feta cheese, coarsely crumbled	250 mL
⅔ cup	PASTENE Grated Parmesan Cheese	150 mL
½ cup	fresh basil, chopped	125 mL
⅓ cup	PASTENE Pitted Olives, sliced	75 mL
⅔ cup	PASTENE Sundried Tomatoes in Oil, drained and chopped	150 mL
⅓ cup	PASTENE Extra Light Olive Oil for frying	75 mL
	all-purpose flour	
	PASTENE Extra Light Olive Oil	

- Grease a baking pan (6 x 10 in./ 15 x 25 cm) with olive oil. Set aside.
- Bring chicken stock and salt to a boil. Add cornmeal a little at time, stirring constantly. Simmer, stirring, for 12 to 15 minutes.
- Remove from heat. Stir in cheeses, basil, olives and sundried tomatoes. Press polenta mixture firmly into prepared pan and refrigerate 3 hours or until firm.
- Cut chilled polenta into 16 wedges. Toss polenta in flour, shaking off excess. Fry in oil until browned and crisp on both sides; drain on paper towels. Serve hot.

BOCCONCINI PIZZA
with Pesto

makes 16 pieces

½	jar (8½ fl. oz/265 mL) PASTENE Italian Bruschetta, drained	1
2	round pizza crusts (6 in./15 cm)	2
3 tbsp	PASTENE Pesto Basil Sauce	45 mL
3-4	balls of Bocconcini cheese	3-4
	PASTENE Extra Virgin Olive Oil	
	dried oregano	

- Preheat oven to 475°F (250°C). Brush 2 pizza pans with olive oil. Place pizza crusts on pans.
- Spread pesto sauce evenly over crust. Slice Bocconcini and arrange over pizza. Top with Bruschetta. Drizzle with olive oil and sprinkle with oregano.
- Bake 10-15 minutes or until crust is golden brown. Cut each pizza in 8 triangles. Serve as an appetizer.

BAKED TOMATOES
with Mushrooms

4 servings

4	medium tomatoes	4
3 tbsp	PASTENE Pure Olive Oil	45 mL
1	onion, chopped	1
2	garlic cloves, chopped	2
1	can (15 oz) PASTENE Broken Straw Mushrooms, or ½ lb (250 g) fresh mushrooms, chopped	1
1 tbsp	fresh parsley, chopped	15 mL
1 tbsp	PASTENE Tomato Paste	15 mL
¼ cup	35% cream	60 mL
¼ cup	PASTENE Grated Romano Cheese	60 mL
¼ cup	PASTENE Flavored Bread Crumbs	60 mL
	PASTENE Pure Olive Oil	
	salt and pepper	

- Preheat oven to 400°F (200°C).
- Using sharp knife, cut tops from tomatoes. Spoon out most of flesh; chop flesh and season to taste. Set aside.
- Heat oil in saucepan over medium heat. Add onion and garlic; cook 4 minutes. Stir in mushrooms, parsley and tomato pulp; season well with salt and pepper. Increase heat to high and cook 6 minutes.
- Stir in tomato paste and cook 2 minutes. Add cream, stir and cook another 4 minutes. Stir in cheese.
- Fill tomato shells with mushroom mixture and top with breadcrumbs. Drizzle with a few drops of oil. Bake 20 minutes. Serve immediately.

FRESH ASPARAGUS
with Vinaigrette

4 servings

2	bunches of asparagus, pared, tough ends trimmed	2
2	egg yolks	2
1 tsp	Dijon mustard	5 mL
4 tbsp	PASTENE Garlic Vinegar	60 mL
1 tbsp	fresh parsley, chopped	15 mL
4	PASTENE Anchovy Fillets in Oil, chopped	4
⅔ cup	PASTENE Extra Virgin Olive Oil	150 mL
⅓ cup	PASTENE Roasted Peppers, chopped	75 mL
¼ cup	PASTENE Grated Parmesan Cheese (optional)	60 mL
	salt and pepper	

- Place asparagus in boiling salted water and cook 7 minutes or until tender. Cool under cold running water, drain and arrange on serving platter.

- Mix egg yolks, mustard, vinegar, parsley and anchovies in a medium bowl. Add oil in thin stream, whisking constantly. Season to taste with salt and pepper and pour over asparagus. Garnish with chopped roasted peppers. Sprinkle with cheese if desired, and serve.

BAKED ROMANO
with Sundried Tomatoes

6 servings

1 tbsp	PASTENE Pure Olive Oil	15 mL
2 cups	PASTENE Grated Romano Cheese	500 mL
¾ cup	PASTENE Sundried Tomatoes in Oil, drained and chopped	175 mL
4	eggs, lightly beaten	4
1 tbsp	fresh oregano, chopped	15 mL
2	garlic cloves, minced	2
¼ cup	35% cream	60 mL

- Preheat oven to 350°F (180°C).
- Grease with olive oil 6 ramekins, or small baking dishes each with ⅓-cup (75 mL) capacity.
- Mix cheese, tomatoes, eggs, oregano, garlic, and cream in large bowl until well blended. Divide equally among ramekins.
- Cover ramekins with foil. Place in baking dish with enough boiling water to come halfway up the sides of ramekins. Bake 30 minutes.
- Remove foil, and place under broiler until tops are golden brown. Serve hot as a first course.

NEAPOLITAN TOMATO
Soufflé

4 servings

½ lb	PASTENE Spaghetti	250 g
2 tbsp	PASTENE Pure Olive Oil	30 mL
2 tbsp	all-purpose flour	30 mL
1 cup	PASTENE Italian Peeled Tomatoes, drained and crushed	250 mL
⅔ cup	PASTENE Grated Parmesan Cheese	150 mL
½ tsp	paprika	2 mL
½ tsp	salt	2 mL
3	eggs yolks	3
	freshly ground pepper	

- Cook pasta in boiling salted water for 10 minutes or until al dente; drain and reserve.
- Preheat oven to 350°F (180°C).
- Heat oil over medium heat, add flour, and stir until well blended. Gradually add tomatoes, stirring constantly. Bring to a boil and let simmer 2 minutes. Add cheese, paprika, salt and pepper. Stir in spaghetti.
- Beat eggs yolks until thick and lemon-colored. Add tomato-spaghetti mixture to egg yolks and stir gently to mix.
- Turn mixture into greased baking dish. Bake 15 minutes or until firm. Serve immediately.

ARTICHOKES
in Lemon Dressing

4 servings

1	can (14 fl. oz/398 mL) PASTENE Artichoke Hearts, well drained	1
3 tbsp	fresh lemon juice	45 mL
2 tbsp	PASTENE Pure Olive Oil	30 mL
1	garlic clove, minced	1
	salt and pepper	

- Refrigerate artichoke hearts until chilled.
- Meanwhile, mix lemon juice, olive oil, garlic, salt and pepper to taste, to make dressing. Refrigerate, covered until ready to serve.
- Pour dressing over artichokes just before serving.

THREE-PEPPER
Pizza

makes 12 pieces

1 tbsp	PASTENE Pure Olive Oil	15 mL
1	cooked pizza crust (6 x 8 in./15 x 20 cm)	1
½	red bell pepper, chopped	½
½	orange bell pepper, chopped	½
½	yellow bell pepper, chopped	½
1	medium onion, chopped	1
1 cup	grated Mozzarella cheese	250 mL
½	jar (8½ fl. oz/265 mL) PASTENE Italian Bruschetta	½
1 tbsp	dried oregano	15 mL
1 tbsp	fresh basil, chopped	15 mL
	salt and pepper	

- Preheat oven to 475°F (250°C). Brush pizza pan with olive oil. Place pizza crust on pan.
- Heat olive oil in skillet. Add peppers and onion and cook 5 minutes over medium-high heat, stirring occasionally. Season to taste with salt and pepper. Remove from heat and set aside.
- Sprinkle pepper mixture and cheese over pizza shell. Dot with Bruschetta. Sprinkle with oregano. Bake 10-15 minutes or until crust is golden brown. Sprinkle with fresh basil and serve immediately.

CLAM-STUFFED
Zucchini

makes about 16 pieces

2	medium zucchini	2
1 tbsp	PASTENE Pure Olive Oil	15 mL
1	small onion, finely chopped	1
1	garlic clove, chopped	1
1	can (10.5 oz/142 g) PASTENE Baby Clams, drained	1
1	can (14 oz/398 mL) PASTENE Italian Peeled Tomatoes, drained and finely chopped	1
¼ cup	PASTENE Grated Parmesan Cheese	60 mL
1 tbsp	fresh chives, chopped	15 mL
¼ cup	PASTENE Flavored Bread Crumbs	60 mL
1	jar (5 oz/170 mL) PASTENE Marinated Artichokes, drained	1
	salt and pepper	

• Preheat oven to 350°F (180°C).

• Cut zucchini crosswise in slices ½ inch (1 cm) thick. Discard ends. With a melon baller or small spoon, hollow out each slice to make a cup shape. Set aside.

• Heat oil in skillet over medium heat. Cook onion and garlic 4 minutes. Stir in clams and chopped tomatoes. Season with salt and pepper. Cook 2 minutes.

• Add cheese and chives. Cook 4 minutes. Fill zucchini cups with clam mixture. Sprinkle with bread crumbs. Bake 5 minutes, then turn on broiler element and broil until golden. Serve hot with PASTENE marinated artichokes.

Cut zucchini crosswise in slices ½ inch (1 cm) thick.

With a melon baller or small spoon, hollow out each slice to make a cup shape.

Heat oil in skillet over medium heat. Cook onion and garlic 4 minutes. Stir in clams and chopped tomatoes. Cook 2 minutes.

Add cheese and chives. Cook 4 minutes.

Fill zucchini cups with clam mixture.

Sprinkle with bread crumbs. Bake 5 minutes, then broil until golden.

Soups
and
Salads

When it comes to versatility, soups and salads are the shining stars of the cooking repertoire. They can be simple or complicated, low-cal or creamy-rich, light enough to pique the appetite before the main course, or substantial enough to serve as the main meal all on their own.

And when it comes to nutritious ingredients, nothing beats a homemade soup or a crisp, fresh salad. Keep an assortment of Pastene pastas, canned fish, olives and prepared vegetables on hand, along with your favorite Pastene olive oils and wine vinegars, and you will always be ready to whip up mouth-watering soups and salads to please the most discerning palates.

PASTA SALAD
à la Florentine

4 servings

½ lb	PASTENE Farfalle	250 g
2	celery stalks, chopped	2
4 tbsp	mayonnaise	60 mL
⅓ cup	PASTENE Extra Virgin Olive Oil	75 mL
⅓ cup	PASTENE Grated Parmesan Cheese	75 mL
1	cucumber, chopped	1
2 cups	fresh spinach, torn up	500 mL
2 tbsp	PASTENE Wine Vinegar	30 mL
1 tbsp	PASTENE Capers in Vinegar, drained and chopped	15 mL
2 tbsp	fresh parsley, chopped	30 mL
2 tbsp	PASTENE Hot Finger Peppers, sliced	30 mL
	salt and pepper	

- Cook pasta in boiling salted water for 10 minutes, or until al dente. Drain and place in a large bowl.
- Add all remaining ingredients and mix well. Season to taste with salt and pepper, and serve immediately. Garnish with Pastene Pitted Olives, if desired.

WARM PASTA SALAD
with Caper Sauce

4-6 servings

1 lb	PASTENE Fusilli	500 g
⅓ cup	PASTENE Extra Virgin Olive Oil	75 mL
¼ cup	PASTENE Capers in Vinegar, drained and finely chopped	60 mL
1	garlic clove, minced	1
1	dry shallot, minced	1
2 oz	PASTENE Anchovy Fillets in Oil, drained and chopped	48 g
1	can (28 fl. oz/796 mL) PASTENE Diced Tomatoes	1
	PASTENE Grated Parmesan Cheese, for garnish	
	PASTENE Pitted Olives for garnish	
	salt and pepper	

- Cook pasta in salted boiling water for 10 minutes; drain and reserve.
- Heat oil in a saucepan over medium heat. Add capers, garlic, shallot and anchovies. Cook, stirring constantly, 4 minutes.
- Add tomatoes with their juice and bring to broil. Simmer 15 minutes. Serve sauce tossed with pasta, garnished with Parmesan and black olives.

ARTICHOKES
with Balsamic Vinaigrette

4 servings

2	jars (5 oz/170 mL ea.) PASTENE Marinated Artichoke Hearts, well drained	2
⅓ cup	PASTENE Pitted Olives, sliced	75 mL
1 tbsp	fresh chervil, chopped	15 mL
1 tbsp	PASTENE Balsamic Vinegar	15 mL
2 tbsp	PASTENE Extra Virgin Olive Oil	30 mL
½ tsp	fresh lemon juice	2 mL
	salt and pepper	
	PASTENE Roasted Peppers, cut in strips	

- In a bowl, stir together all ingredients until artichokes are well coated. Garnish with roasted red pepper strips.
- Serve immediately, cold, as a side dish or appetizer.

MUSSEL
Soup

6-8 servings

⅓ cup	PASTENE Extra Virgin Olive Oil	75 mL
3½ lbs	fresh mussels, cleaned	1.5 kg
¾ cup	dry white wine	175 mL
4	garlic cloves, chopped	4
4	PASTENE Anchovy Fillets in Oil, finely chopped	4
¼ tsp	crushed red pepper flakes	2 mL
1	can (28 fl. oz/796 mL) PASTENE Italian Tomatoes, diced	1
⅓ cup	fresh parsley, chopped	75 mL
	PASTENE Extra Virgin Olive Oil for garnish (optional)	
	salt and freshly ground black pepper	

• In a skillet, heat half the olive oil over medium-high heat. Add mussels and white wine. Cover and steam over high heat until mussels open. Discard any unopened mussels.

• In a large skillet, heat remaining olive oil and lightly brown the garlic. Stir in the anchovies. Add the cooking liquid from the mussels, tomatoes, pepper flakes and parsley. Simmer for about 20 minutes, uncovered.

• Add the cooked mussels and salt and pepper to taste. Serve in warm soup bowls topped with a drizzle of PASTENE Extra Virgin Olive Oil, if desired.

MESCLUN SALAD
with Pesto Vinaigrette

4-6 servings

Dressing

½ cup	PASTENE Extra Virgin Olive Oil	125 mL
2 tbsp	PASTENE Wine Vinegar	30 mL
1 tsp	salt	5 mL
1 tbsp	PASTENE Pesto Basil Sauce	15 mL
⅛ tsp	freshly ground pepper	0.5 mL
½	head of chicory	½
½	head of Boston lettuce	½
1	radicchio	1
1 cup	lamb's lettuce	250 mL
1 cup	endives, washed and sliced	250 mL

- Beat all dressing ingredients together until thick. Chill.
- Wash and dry lettuces, and tear into bite-size pieces. Combine with sliced endives in salad bowl. Pour dressing over and serve immediately.

GREEN
Salad

4 servings

1	head of lettuce of your choice	1
½ cup	carrots, finely chopped	125 mL
½ cup	red onion, sliced	125 mL

Dressing

1	hard-cooked egg, chopped	1
1 tsp	PASTENE Wine Vinegar	5 mL
2 tsp	PASTENE Extra Virgin Olive Oil	10 mL
1 tbsp	Dijon mustard	15 mL
½ tsp	fresh parsley, chopped	2 mL
	salt and pepper	

- Wash and dry lettuce; tear in small pieces. Combine in salad bowl with carrots and onion.
- In a small bowl, mash egg with a fork. With fork, stir in vinegar, olive oil, mustard, parsley, and salt and pepper to taste. Pour dressing on vegetables, toss and serve immediately.

CREAM OF ARTICHOKE
Soup

8 to 10 servings

½ cup	butter	125 mL
4	medium potatoes, diced	4
3	carrots, diced	3
3	celery stalks, finely chopped	3
1	medium onion, finely chopped	1
8 cups	milk	2 L
3	cans (14 fl. oz/398 mL ea.) PASTENE Artichokes Hearts, drained	3
¼ cup	sherry	60 mL
½ cup	PASTENE Extra Virgin Olive Oil	125 mL
	salt and pepper	

- In a large saucepan, melt the butter. Add vegetables (except artichokes) and cook until tender. Stir in milk, and season with salt and pepper. Bring to a boil. Reduce heat and simmer uncovered for 15 minutes.

- In food processor, puree the artichokes. Add puree to saucepan and cook 5 minutes, stirring occasionally. Add sherry and simmer for another 5 minutes.

- Drizzle each serving with about 1 tbsp (15 mL) extra virgin olive oil and serve hot.

CHEESE AND WALNUT
Salad

4 servings

1	**Boston lettuce**	1
1 tbsp	**PASTENE Wine Vinegar**	15 mL
3 tbsp	**PASTENE Extra Virgin Olive Oil**	45 mL
1	**red apple, cut in julienne strips**	1
⅓ cup	**walnuts, chopped**	75 mL
¾ cup	**seedless red grapes, halved**	175 mL
¼ lb	**Brie cheese, diced**	100 g
2 tbsp	**PASTENE Grated Romano Cheese**	30 mL
	salt	

- Wash the lettuce and dry it well. Tear in bite-size pieces.
- Combine wine vinegar, oil and salt to taste; reserve.
- In a salad bowl, combine lettuce, apple, walnuts, grapes, Brie and Romano. Pour the raspberry dressing over and toss to mix before serving.

ROASTED PEPPER
Soup

4-6 servings

2	cans (28 fl. oz/796 mL ea.) PASTENE Italian Peeled Tomatoes	2
2 cups	chicken stock	500 mL
½ cup	dry white wine	125 mL
2	garlic cloves, minced	2
2 tbsp	fresh basil, chopped	30 mL
¼ tsp	saffron threads	2 mL
1	leek	1
1	jar (5 oz/170 mL) PASTENE Roasted Peppers	1
½ lb	firm-fleshed fish such as halibut, cubed	250 g
	salt	

- Drain tomatoes, reserving juice, and chop tomatoes finely. Place tomatoes in large saucepan with their reserved juice, the chicken stock, wine, garlic, half of the basil and salt to taste.
- Crush saffron threads and add to tomatoes. Cover and bring to a boil over high heat.
- Trim roots and green leaves from leek. Cut white of leek lengthwise and wash carefully to remove any sand. Slice thinly crosswise and add to tomato mixture.
- When mixture returns to a boil, cover and reduce heat to low for 20 minutes. Stir occasionally.
- Drain and chop roasted peppers. Add to tomato mixture. Add fish, cover, and cook 6 to 8 minutes, or until fish flakes with a fork. Serve with remaining chopped fresh basil.

Drain tomatoes, reserving juice, and chop tomatoes finely. Place tomatoes in large saucepan with their reserved juice, the chicken stock, wine, garlic, basil and salt to taste.

Crush saffron threads and add to tomatoes. Cover and bring to a boil over high heat.

Cut white of leek lengthwise and wash carefully to remove any sand. Slice thinly crosswise and add to tomato mixture.

Bring back to a boil, cover and reduce heat to low for 20 minutes. Stir occasionally. Add chopped roasted peppers.

Add fish, cover and cook 6 to 8 minutes, or until fish flakes with a fork. Serve.

CREAMY PASTA
Salad

4 servings

3 cups	cooked PASTENE Fusilli	750 mL
½ cup	PASTENE Diced Tomatoes, well drained	125 mL
24	PASTENE Ripe Olives	24
12	radishes, thinly sliced	12

Dressing

1 tbsp	strong Dijon mustard	15 mL
3 tbsp	mayonnaise	45 mL
2 tbsp	sour cream	30 mL
	juice of 1 lemon	
	salt and pepper	

- Combine pasta, tomatoes, olives and radishes in a salad bowl.
- Stir together ingredients for dressing until smooth. Pour over salad and toss well before serving.

PENNE, ARTICHOKE AND ASPARAGUS
Salad

4 servings

½ lb	PASTENE Penne Rigate	250 g
8	PASTENE Sundried Tomatoes in Oil, drained	8
8	fresh asparagus spears, chopped	8
2	dry shallots, finely chopped	2
1 tsp	fresh thyme, chopped	5 mL
1	garlic clove, minced	1
⅓ cup	PASTENE Extra Virgin Olive Oil	75 mL
3 tbsp	PASTENE Wine Vinegar	45 mL
1	can (14 fl. oz/398 mL) PASTENE Artichoke Hearts, drained and quartered	1
⅓ cup	PASTENE Grated Parmesan Cheese	75 mL
	salt and pepper	

- Cook pasta in boiling salted water for 10 minutes, or until al dente. Drain and reserve.
- Cook sundried tomatoes in boiling salted water for 4 minutes. Drain, chop and reserve. Cook asparagus in boiling salted water for 5 minutes. Drain and reserve.
- In a bowl, combine shallots, thyme, garlic, olive oil, vinegar and artichokes. Add reserved pasta, sundried tomatoes and asparagus and mix well. Add Parmesan and season to taste with salt and pepper. Toss to mix and serve immediately.

MINESTRONE
Sicilian Style

6-8 servings

¼ cup	PASTENE Pure Olive Oil	60 mL
8	celery stalks with leaves, diced	8
3	carrots, diced	3
1	large onion, diced	1
3	medium potatoes, sliced	3
1	can (28 fl. oz/796 mL) PASTENE Italian Peeled Tomatoes, chopped, with juice	1
8 cups	chicken stock	2 L
1 cup	frozen peas	250 mL
¼ lb	PASTENE Spaghetti	110 g
2 tbsp	fresh basil, chopped	30 mL
	PASTENE Grated Parmesan Cheese	
	salt and pepper	

- Heat olive oil in skillet. Add celery, carrots and onion. Cook about 5 minutes, stirring occasionally.
- Add potatoes, tomatoes with juice, and chicken stock. Season with salt and pepper to taste. Cook for 15 minutes.
- Add peas and spaghetti broken in small pieces. Cook 7-8 minutes, or until spaghetti are tender. Add basil and serve with Parmesan cheese on top.

PANCETTA BEAN
Salad

4 servings

1	can (14 oz/398 mL) PASTENE White Kidney Beans	1
1 tbsp	PASTENE Wine Vinegar	15 mL
3 tbsp	PASTENE Extra Virgin Olive Oil	45 mL
⅓ cup	pancetta (Italian bacon), diced and cooked	75 mL
1 tsp	orange zest, grated	5 mL
1 tbsp	fresh parsley, chopped freshly ground pepper	15 mL

- Thoroughly drain and rinse beans in a colander. Put in a bowl.
- Add wine vinegar and toss to mix. Add olive oil and toss again. Add pancetta (or bacon), orange zest, parsley and pepper to taste. Mix until combined.
- Chill at least one hour before serving.

SEAFOOD AND SPINACH
Salad

4 servings

1 tbsp	PASTENE Extra Virgin Olive Oil	15 mL
12	sea scallops, cut in two	12
8	large shrimps, peeled and deveined	8
2	dry shallots, chopped	2
1 lb	spinach leaves	500 g
1 cup	pea shoots (or alfalfa sprouts)	250 mL
¼ cup	PASTENE Extra Virgin Olive Oil	60 mL
2 tbsp	PASTENE Balsamic Vinegar	30 mL
½ cup	PASTENE Roasted Peppers, cubed	125 mL
	salt and pepper	

- Heat 1 tbsp/15 mL olive oil in a skillet over medium-high heat. Add scallops and shrimps and cook 2-3 minutes. Add shallots, turn scallops and shrimps, and cook another 2 minutes.
- Wash spinach leaves, discarding tough stems.
- In a salad bowl, combine spinach, pea shoots (or alfafa sprouts), ¼ cup/60 mL of olive oil, vinegar and roasted pepper. Season to taste with salt and pepper and add scallops and shrimps. Serve immediately.

TOMATO AND BLACK OLIVE
Salad

4-6 servings

8	ripe tomatoes	8
1	red onion, sliced	1
2 cups	PASTENE Ripe Olives	500 mL
1 cup	fresh basil, chopped	250 mL

Dressing

¼ cup	PASTENE Extra Virgin Olive Oil	60 mL
1½ tbsp	PASTENE Balsamic Vinegar	22 mL
½ tsp	sugar	2 mL
1 tbsp	grainy-style mustard	15 mL

- Quarter tomatoes; slice each quarter in half. In a bowl, toss tomatoes with onion, olives and basil.
- Combine dressing ingredients in a jar with a tight-fitting lid. Shake dressing vigorously and pour over tomatoes. Serve immediately.

RICE SALAD
à la Pastene

4-6 servings

2	green onions, chopped	2
4 tbsp	PASTENE Extra Virgin Olive Oil	60 mL
2 cups	PASTENE Italian Arborio Rice, cooked	500 mL
1 tbsp	PASTENE Wine Vinegar	15 mL
1 can	(14 fl. oz/398 mL) PASTENE Artichokes Hearts, drained	1
1 can	(14 fl. oz/398 mL) PASTENE Hearts of Palm, drained	1
⅓ cup	PASTENE Roasted Peppers, cubed	75 mL
2 tsp	fresh lemon juice	10 mL
¼ tsp	Dijon mustard	2 mL
1	garlic clove, minced	1
¼ tsp	fresh thyme, chopped	2 mL
4	hard-boiled eggs, sliced	4
	PASTENE Anchovy Fillets in Oil	
	fresh thyme	

- In a large skillet, stir-fry green onions in half the olive oil for 1 minute. Add cooked rice and stir to coat with oil. Reserve.
- While rice cools, stir together remaining olive oil with vinegar, artichoke hearts, hearts of palm, red pepper, lemon juice, mustard, garlic and thyme. Season to taste with salt and pepper.
- Pour mixture over rice and mix well. Garnish with egg slices, anchovies and sprigs of thyme.

PASTENE CAESAR
Salad

4 servings

4	**PASTENE Anchovy Fillets in Oil**, chopped	4
3 tbsp	**PASTENE Wine Vinegar**	45 mL
2	garlic cloves, chopped	2
1 tbsp	**PASTENE Capers in Vinegar**, chopped	15 mL
1	egg yolk	1
½ cup	**PASTENE Extra Virgin Olive Oil**	125 mL
½ cup	**PASTENE Grated Parmesan Cheese**	125 mL
2	heads of Romaine lettuce, washed and dried	2
4	slices of crisp cooked bacon, diced	4
½ cup	croutons (optional)	125 mL
	salt and pepper	

- For the dressing, mix anchovies, vinegar, garlic, capers and egg yolk in a bowl. Add oil in a thin stream, whisking constantly. Season to taste with salt and pepper. Whisk in half the cheese.
- Tear lettuce leaves into small pieces; place in salad bowl. Pour dressing over and toss to coat thoroughly. Add bacon and remaining cheese, and toss again. Serve with croutons, if desired.

CLAM
Chowder

4 servings

1 tbsp	PASTENE Pure Olive Oil	15 mL
1	onion, finely chopped	1
1	celery stalk, diced	1
1	green pepper, diced	1
2	potatoes, peeled and diced	2
½ tsp	dried fennel seed, crushed	2 mL
2	cans (10.5 oz/142 g ea.) PASTENE Baby Clams	2
3 cups	chicken or vegetable stock, heated	750 mL
½ cup	35% cream	125 mL
1 tbsp	fresh chives, chopped	15 mL
	paprika	
	salt and pepper	

• Heat oil in saucepan. Add all the vegetables, cover and cook 5 minutes over low heat, until onion is softened.

• Add fennel. Drain juice from clams into the saucepan, reserving the clams. Add stock and season to taste with salt and pepper. Bring to a boil.

• Reduce heat and simmer 15 minutes uncovered over medium heat or until potatoes are cooked.

• Stir in cream, chives and reserved clams; season again with salt and pepper to taste and simmer 5 minutes. Serve garnished with a sprinkling of paprika.

Heat oil in saucepan. Add all the vegetables, cover and cook 5 minutes over low heat, until onion is softened.

Add fennel. Drain juice from clams into the saucepan, reserving the clams.

Add stock and season to taste with salt and pepper. Bring to a boil.

Reduce heat and simmer 15 minutes uncovered over medium heat or until potatoes are cooked. Stir in cream and chives.

Add clams; season again with salt and pepper to taste, and simmer 5 minutes. Serve.

VEGETARIAN SALAD
with Black Olives

4-6 servings

1	can (14 fl. oz/398 mL) PASTENE Artichoke Hearts, drained and chopped	1
1	can (14 fl. oz/398 mL) PASTENE Hearts of Palm, drained and sliced	1
1	can (14 fl. oz/398 mL) PASTENE Pitted Black Olives	1
1	red pepper, finely diced	1
1	yellow pepper, diced	1

Dressing

1 tsp	salt	5 mL
½ tsp	dry mustard	2 mL
¼ tsp	paprika	1 mL
½ tsp	celery salt	2 mL
2	garlic cloves, minced	2
⅓ cup	PASTENE Pure Olive Oil	75 mL
2 tbsp	PASTENE Garlic Vinegar	30 mL

- Combine ingredients for the dressing and refrigerate until ready to serve.
- Place vegetables in a salad bowl and pour dressing over. Toss to combine. Serve immediately.

PALM HEARTS AND ARTICHOKES
with Pesto Dressing

4 servings

1	can (14 fl. oz/398 mL) PASTENE Hearts of Palm, drained and sliced (½ in./1 cm thick)	1
1	can (14 fl. oz/398 mL) PASTENE Artichoke Hearts, drained and halved	1
1 tbsp	strong Dijon mustard	15 mL
1	egg yolk	1
3 tbsp	PASTENE Garlic Vinegar	45 mL
1 tbsp	PASTENE Pesto Basil Sauce	15 mL
½ cup	PASTENE Pure Olive Oil	125 mL
1 tbsp	fresh parsley, chopped	15 mL
	salt and pepper	

- Arrange hearts of palm and artichoke hearts on a deep platter; set aside.
- Combine mustard with egg yolk, salt and pepper to taste. Whisk in wine vinegar and pesto sauce. Add oil in thin stream, whisking constantly until thick.
- Stir in parsley, pour over vegetables and let marinate 15 minutes, stirring twice. Serve on lettuce.

BROCCOLI
Salad

4 servings

3 cups	broccoli florets	750 mL
1	onion, sliced and separated into rings	1
½ cup	sliced mushrooms	125 mL
¼ lb	Feta cheese, crumbled	100 g
1	lemon	1
¼ cup	PASTENE Extra Virgin Olive Oil	60 mL
1	garlic clove, minced	1
1 tsp	fresh oregano, chopped	5 mL
¼ tsp	pepper	1 mL

- Drop broccoli in rapidly boiling water over high heat. As soon as water returns to a boil, remove broccoli. Drain and chill.
- When cold, add onion, mushrooms and cheese.
- Squeeze the lemon juice into a blender. Add olive oil, garlic, oregano and pepper, and process until smooth. Pour over broccoli mixture, toss and serve immediately.

GAZPACHO

6-8 servings

1	can (28 fl. oz/796 mL) PASTENE Italian Peeled Tomatoes	1
3	cucumbers, peeled, seeded and chopped	3
2	red onions, chopped	2
2	garlic cloves, chopped	2
1	green pepper, chopped	1
¼ cup	PASTENE Wine Vinegar	60 mL
1 cup	PASTENE Flavored Bread Crumbs	250 mL
¼ cup	PASTENE Extra Virgin Olive Oil	60 mL
1 cup	chicken stock	250 mL
2 tbsp	PASTENE Balsamic Vinegar	30 mL
2 tsp	Tabasco sauce	10 mL
	garlic croutons	
	fresh coriander	

- In a blender or food processor, blend together all ingredients except croutons and coriander, in batches if necessary.
- Refrigerate at least 6 hours or overnight. Serve chilled, sprinkled with garlic croutons and fresh coriander.

PASTA SALAD
with Tuna

4 servings

8 oz	PASTENE Fusilli	250 g
1	can (6 oz/198 g) PASTENE Light Meat Tuna (Tonno) in oil	1
10 oz	green beans, cut up and cooked	300 g
½ cup	PASTENE Pitted Olives, sliced	125 mL
2 tbsp	fresh chives, chopped	30 mL
3 tbsp	PASTENE Extra Virgin Olive Oil	45 mL
1 tbsp	PASTENE Wine Vinegar	15 mL
	salt and pepper	

- Cook pasta in boiling salted water until al dente; drain and place in a large bowl.
- Drain tuna and crumble. Add to pasta, along with green beans, olives and chives.
- In a jar with a tight-fitting lid, shake together oil, vinegar, salt and pepper. Toss with pasta and serve immediately.

TUNA
Salad

4 servings

1	can (6 oz/198 g) PASTENE Light Meat Tuna (Tonno), drained	1
1	carrot, grated	1
2 tsp	PASTENE Balsamic Vinegar	10 mL
1 tbsp	PASTENE Extra Virgin Olive Oil	15 mL
2 tbsp	PASTENE Capers in Vinegar, drained	30 mL
2	green onions, sliced	2

- In a bowl, flake tuna with a fork. Add carrot, vinegar, olive oil, capers and green onions. Toss well before serving.
- Can also be used as a sandwich filling.

LEEK AND BASIL SOUP

4-6 servings

1 tbsp	PASTENE Pure Olive Oil	15 mL
2	leeks, washed, white part sliced	2
1	red onion, chopped	1
2 tbsp	PASTENE Pesto Basil Sauce	30 mL
1	garlic clove, finely minced	1
2	potatoes, peeled and sliced	2
4 cups	heated chicken stock	1 L
	salt and pepper	

- In a large saucepan, heat oil over medium-low heat. Add leeks and onion. Cook 5 minutes.
- Add remaining ingredients, season to taste with salt and pepper, and bring to boil. Cook at least 20 minutes over low heat, stirring occasionally, until potatoes are tender. Serve hot.

FOUR BEAN
Salad

12 servings

1	can (14 oz/398 mL) PASTENE Chick Peas	1
1	can (14 oz/398 mL) PASTENE White Kidney Beans	1
1	can (14 oz/398 mL) PASTENE Red Kidney Beans	1
1	can (14 oz/398 mL) PASTENE Black Beans	1
¼ cup	fresh Italian parsley, chopped	60 mL
1	onion, finely chopped	1
3	celery stalks, sliced	3
¼ cup	PASTENE Wine Vinegar	60 mL
⅓ cup	PASTENE Extra Virgin Olive Oil	75 mL
1 tbsp	Dijon mustard	15 mL
1	pinch of tarragon, dried and crushed	1
	salt and pepper	

- Drain and rinse all 4 types of beans in a colander. When well drained, combine beans in a large bowl with parsley, onion and celery.
- In a jar with a tight-fitting lid, combine vinegar, olive oil, mustard and tarragon, and shake well. Pour over bean mixture and toss. Season with salt and pepper to taste and toss again.
- Cover and chill well before serving.

SHRIMP
Minestrone

4-6 servings

¼ cup	PASTENE Extra Virgin Olive Oil	60 mL
½ cup	red onion, chopped	125 mL
6 cups	chicken stock	1.5 L
1	can (14 fl. oz/398 mL) PASTENE Diced Tomatoes	1
½ cup	diced carrots	125 mL
1 cup	diced green cabbage	250 mL
1 cup	diced zucchini	250 mL
2 tbsp	PASTENE Pesto Basil Sauce	30 mL
12	medium shrimps, peeled and deveined	12
	salt and pepper	

- In a large pot, heat olive oil over medium heat and add onion; cook for 3 minutes.
- Add chicken stock, tomatoes with juice and carrots. Cook 10 minutes.
- Add cabbage and zucchini and continue cooking 10 minutes. Add pesto and shrimps and cook over medium heat 7-8 minutes. Season to taste with salt and pepper and serve immediately.

OLD-FASHIONED TOMATO
Soup

4-6 servings

1 cup	vegetable stock	250 mL
1 cup	chicken stock	250 mL
2 cups	tomato juice	500 mL
1 cup	PASTENE "Kitchen Ready" Ground Tomatoes	250 mL
⅓ cup	red onions, chopped	75 mL
1	garlic clove, chopped	1
⅓ cup	PASTENE Italian Arborio Rice	75 mL
	salt and pepper	

- Mix all ingredients in a large saucepan and bring to a boil. Turn heat to low and simmer, covered, for 30 minutes.
- Remove from heat and let cool. Puree, in batches if necessary, in blender or food processor.
- Return to pan and simmer another 5 minutes before serving.

ROQUEFORT
Salad

4 servings

1	large romaine lettuce, washed and dried	1
1	bunch of watercress, washed, dried and stems trimmed	1
1	cucumber, peeled, seeded and sliced	1
4	PASTENE Hearts of Palm, sliced	4
½ cup	Roquefort cheese	125 mL
¼ cup	PASTENE Extra Virgin Olive Oil	60 mL
2 tbsp	dry white wine	30 mL
2 tbsp	PASTENE Garlic Vinegar	30 mL
¼ cup	PASTENE Grated Parmesan Cheese	60 mL
½ cup	croutons	125 mL
	fresh lemon juice	
	salt and pepper	

- Tear lettuce leaves into small pieces and place in salad bowl. Add watercress, cucumber and hearts of palm.
- Place Roquefort cheese in second bowl. Add olive oil and mix until well blended. Add wine, vinegar and lemon juice according to taste; season with salt and pepper and mix well.
- Pour dressing over salad, add croutons and toss. Sprinkle with Parmesan cheese and serve immediately.

Tear lettuce leaves into small pieces and place in salad bowl. Add watercress, cucumber and hearts of palm.

Place Roquefort cheese in another bowl, add olive oil and mix until well blended.

Add wine, vinegar and lemon juice to taste; season with salt and pepper and mix well.

Pour dressing over salad, add croutons and toss.

Sprinkle with Parmesan cheese and serve immediately.

HEALTHY ITALIAN
Soup

4-6 servings

1 tbsp	PASTENE Extra Light Olive Oil	15 mL
2	medium onions, halved and sliced	2
½ cup	pancetta (Italian bacon), diced	125 mL
4 cups	chicken stock	1 L
1	can (28 fl. oz/796 mL) PASTENE Diced Tomatoes	1
2	bay leaves	2
3	parsley sprigs	3
3	thyme sprigs	3
¾ cup	PASTENE Stelline	175 mL
2 cups	rapini, chopped	500 mL
1	can (14 oz/398 mL) PASTENE White Kidney Beans, drained	1
	PASTENE Grated Parmesan Cheese, (optional)	

- Heat olive oil in a large soup pot over medium heat. Add onions and cook 5 minutes. Add pancetta and cook until lightly colored.

- Add chicken stock, tomatoes, bay leaves, parsley and thyme. Cook about 10 minutes over medium heat.

- Add pasta and rapini. Cook 6-7 minutes. Add white kidney beans and cook 4-5 minutes or until beans are heated through. Serve with grated Parmesan, if desired.

RAPINI AND RICE
Salad

4 servings

1 cup	PASTENE Italian Arborio Rice	250 mL
8	PASTENE Sundried Tomatoes in Oil, drained	8
1	head of rapini, washed and coarsely chopped	1
1	red onion, chopped	1
1	yellow bell pepper, chopped	1
1	green bell pepper, chopped	1
1	red bell pepper, chopped	1
⅓ cup	PASTENE Extra Virgin Olive Oil	75 mL
3 tbsp	PASTENE Balsamic Vinegar	45 mL
	salt and pepper	

- Cook rice in boiling salted water for 20 minutes, or until just tender; drain and reserve.
- Cook sundried tomatoes in boiling salted water for about 4 minutes. Drain and let cool.
- Cook rapini in boiling salted water for about 4 minutes.
- In a bowl, combine red onion and bell peppers. Add cold rice and rapini and toss well. Season to taste with salt and pepper. Add olive oil and vinegar and mix well. Serve immediately.

Pasta and Risotto

Lately, we've been hearing a lot of advice from health and diet advocates about the importance of eating less fat and sugar, and more healthy carbohydrates–the kind found in grains, beans, pasta, fruits and vegetables.

Scientists have proven that certain compounds found in some natural foods–including olive oil, garlic and cooked tomatoes–can actually protect us from disease.

So this chapter will be of special interest to people concerned with good health as well good taste. It's filled with the wonderful flavors of creamy risottos, quick and healthy pasta sauces, and other delicious, nutritious dishes made even easier with Pastene's convenient tomato products, pastas, and canned vegetables.

TOMATO AND MUSHROOM
Risotto

4 servings

1½ cups	PASTENE "Kitchen Ready" Ground Tomatoes	375 mL
3 cups	chicken stock, heated	750 mL
2 tbsp	PASTENE Pure Olive Oil	30 mL
1	can (15-oz) PASTENE Broken Straw Mushrooms, drained	1
¾ lb	mushrooms, quartered	350 g
1	onion, finely chopped	1
2	garlic cloves, minced	2
1½ cups	PASTENE Italian Arborio Rice	375 mL
½ cup	dry white wine	125 mL
⅓ cup	PASTENE Pitted Olives, sliced	75 mL
2 tbsp	chopped fresh parsley	30 mL
½ cup	PASTENE Grated Parmesan Cheese	125 mL
	fresh parsley	

- Combine tomatoes with chicken stock and bring to a boil; cover and keep hot.
- Heat olive oil in large heavy pan over medium-high heat and cook mushrooms until all liquid has evaporated; remove from pan and reserve.
- In the same pan, cook onion and garlic for 4 minutes, stirring constantly and adding more oil if necessary to prevent sticking.
- When onions are soft, add rice; stir to coat with oil. Add wine, stir and cook over medium-low heat, uncovered, until wine is absorbed. Ladle in ½ cup (125 mL) heated tomato stock mixture and cook, stirring constantly, over low heat until liquid is absorbed.
- Continue adding stock mixture gradually, stirring until absorbed before each addition. Cook 15-20 minutes or until rice is tender. Stir in reserved mushrooms (keep a few pieces for garnish), olives, parsley, and Parmesan. Serve immediately garnished with parsley and mushrooms.

FETTUCINE
with Red Clam Sauce

4-6 servings

14 oz	PASTENE Fettuccine	400 g
2 tbsp	PASTENE Extra Virgin Olive Oil	30 mL
3	garlic cloves, minced	3
1	small onion, chopped	1
1 tbsp	PASTENE Tomato Paste	15 mL
1	can (28 fl. oz/796 mL) PASTENE Italian Peeled Tomatoes, chopped	1
⅓ cup	dry white wine	75 mL
2	cans (10.5 oz/142 g) PASTENE Baby Clams	2
2 tbsp	chopped fresh chives	30 mL
	salt and pepper	

- Cook pasta in boiling salted water for 10 minutes or until al dente; drain and reserve.

- Meanwhile, heat oil in a skillet and cook garlic and onion for 4 minutes. Add tomato paste, tomatoes, wine, and the juice from 1 can of clams. Season with salt and pepper to taste.

- Simmer for 30 minutes. Add clams (discard juice from 2nd can) and chives. Simmer for 5 minutes, then serve over hot cooked pasta and serve immediately.

SPAGHETTI
Carbonara

4-6 servings

16 oz	PASTENE Spaghetti	500 g
8	slices of bacon, diced	8
4	eggs, lightly beaten	4
4 tbsp	15% cream	60 mL
2 tbsp	PASTENE Extra Virgin Olive Oil	30 mL
¼ cup	PASTENE Grated Parmesan Cheese	60 mL
2 tbsp	chopped fresh parsley salt and pepper	30 mL

- Cook spaghetti in boiling, salted water until al dente. Drain and keep hot.
- Meanwhile, cook bacon in a skillet over medium heat until crisp. Drain and reserve.
- In a bowl, combine eggs and cream. Season to taste with salt and pepper.
- Heat olive oil in a skillet. Stir in reserved spaghetti, bacon, egg mixture and Parmesan. Mix very well and serve immediately, garnished with parsley.

WHITE KIDNEY BEANS
with Tomatoes

4-6 servings

2	cans (14 fl. oz/398 mL ea.) PASTENE White Kidney Beans	2
1 tbsp	PASTENE Pure Olive Oil	15 mL
1	large onion, halved and sliced	1
1	can (28 fl. oz/796 mL) PASTENE Italian Peeled Tomatoes, chopped	1
1	green pepper, sliced	1
1 tsp	chopped fresh thyme	5 mL
8	fresh sage leaves	8
	salt and pepper	

- Drain and rinse kidney beans through a colander. Set aside.

- Heat olive oil in a skillet over medium-high heat. Add onion and cook for 2 minutes. Add tomatoes, season with salt and pepper to taste and cook over medium heat about 15 minutes.

- Add green pepper, thyme, and sage. Cook another 3 minutes. Add white kidney beans and simmer 5 minutes. Serve as a side dish.

CHICKEN
Risotto

4 servings

1½ tbsp	PASTENE Extra Virgin Olive Oil	23 mL
4	skinless, boneless chicken breast halves, sliced	4
2	red onions, chopped	2
1	dry shallot, finely chopped	1
2	garlic cloves, minced	2
1 tsp	chopped fresh thyme	5 mL
1½ cups	PASTENE Italian Arborio Rice	375 mL
4 cups	chicken stock, heated	1 liter
1 tbsp	PASTENE Balsamic Vinegar	15 mL
⅓ cup	PASTENE Grated Parmesan Cheese	75 mL
2	eggs, beaten	2
8	PASTENE Italian Peeled Tomatoes, drained and finely chopped	8

- Preheat oven to 350°F (180°C).

- In a saucepan, heat 1 tbsp (15 mL) oil over medium-high heat. Add chicken and cook 5-8 minutes. Remove chicken from saucepan and reserve.

- Heat remaining oil in the same saucepan. Add onions, shallot, garlic, and thyme and cook over medium heat, stirring constantly, for 4 minutes. Add rice and mix well.

- Add chicken stock 1 cup (250 mL) at a time, stirring and cooking until all liquid is absorbed before adding more. Add vinegar. Once all liquid is absorbed, continue cooking over low heat until rice is barely tender.

- Stir in reserved cooked chicken, Parmesan, eggs, and tomatoes. Mix well and cook until heated through. Serve immediately.

In a saucepan, heat 1 tbsp (15 mL) oil over medium-high heat. Add chicken and cook 5-8 minutes. Remove chicken from saucepan and reserve.

Heat remaining oil in the same saucepan. Add onions, shallot, garlic, and thyme and cook over medium heat, stirring constantly, for 4 minutes.

Add rice and mix well.

*Add chicken stock 1 cup
(250 mL) at a time, stirring
and cooking until all liquid
is absorbed before adding
more. Add vinegar.*

*Stir in reserved cooked
chicken, Parmesan, eggs, and
tomatoes. Mix well and cook
until heated through.*

MEAT BALLS
Sicilian Style

4 servings

1 lb	ground beef	500 g
1	egg	1
½ cup	PASTENE Flavored Bread Crumbs	125 mL
2 tbsp	PASTENE Grated Parmesan Cheese	30 mL
½ tsp	each, salt and pepper	2 mL
1 tbsp	chopped fresh parsley	15 mL
1	large red onion, finely chopped	1
¼ cup	PASTENE Pure Olive Oil	60 mL
1 can	(28 fl. oz/796 mL) PASTENE Diced Ready Spiced Tomatoes	1
2 tbsp	PASTENE Tomato Paste	30 mL
1 tsp	sugar	5 mL
1 tbsp	PASTENE Balsamic Vinegar	15 mL
1	pinch each, nutmeg and cinnamon	1
	PASTENE Pasta of your choice	

- Mix thoroughly in a bowl: beef, egg, bread crumbs, Parmesan, salt and pepper, parsley, and onion. Shape mixture into balls about 1 inch (2.5 cm) in diameter.

- Heat olive oil in a skillet over medium-high heat. Brown meat balls on all sides and set aside.

- To the oil left in the skillet, add diced tomatoes, tomato paste, sugar, balsamic vinegar, nutmeg, and cinnamon. Cover tightly, and cook over medium-low heat for 15 minutes.

- Add the meatballs to the sauce and cook slowly for another 20 minutes. Serve with your favorite Pastene pasta.

LINGUINE
with Black Olives

4-6 servings

16 oz	**PASTENE Linguine**	500 g
5	eggs	5
½ cup	35% cream	125 mL
1 cup	**PASTENE Grated Parmesan Cheese**	250 mL
2 tbsp	**chopped fresh parsley**	30 mL
¼ cup	**pitted black olives, minced**	60 mL
2 tbsp	**PASTENE Extra Virgin Olive Oil**	30 mL
2	**garlic cloves, minced**	2
1	**can (14 fl. oz/398 mL) PASTENE Pitted Olives, sliced, drained**	1
	salt and pepper	

• Cook pasta in boiling, salted water until al dente. Drain and keep hot.

• Meanwhile, beat together eggs, cream, Parmesan, and parsley. Add olive spread and mix well. Reserve.

• Heat oil in a skillet over medium heat. Add garlic and cook 3 minutes, until soft. Add pasta, egg and cheese mixture, and olives. Over medium-low heat, toss 3-4 minutes until eggs thicken and coat spaghetti. Season to taste and serve immediately.

FETTUCINI
alla Melanzane

4 servings

16 oz	PASTENE Fettuccine	500 g
3	small eggplants	3
2 tbsp	PASTENE Pure Olive Oil	30 mL
2	garlic cloves, minced	2
1	can (28 fl. oz/796 mL) PASTENE Italian Peeled Tomatoes, chopped	1
5-7	fresh basil leaves	5-7
	salt and pepper	
	PASTENE Extra Light Olive Oil for frying	
	PASTENE Grated Parmesan Cheese	

- Cook pasta in boiling salted water for 10 minutes or until al dente; drain and keep hot.
- Meanwhile, wash eggplants and slice thinly. Sprinkle with salt and let stand for 10 minutes.
- Heat olive oil in a skillet over medium heat. Cook garlic until soft, but not brown. Add tomatoes, basil, and salt and pepper to taste. Simmer for 12-15 minutes.
- Meanwhile, rinse eggplant slices and pat dry. Heat a thin layer of olive oil in a second skillet over medium-high heat. Fry eggplant slices until brown and crisp on both sides, adding more oil if necessary.
- Mix tomato-basil sauce with eggplant and hot pasta. Sprinkle with Parmesan and serve immediately.

Wash eggplants and slice thinly.

Sprinkle eggplants slices with salt and let stand for 10 minutes.

Heat olive oil in a skillet over medium heat. Cook garlic until soft, but not brown. Add tomatoes, basil, and salt and pepper to taste. Simmer for 12-15 minutes.

Rinse eggplant slices and pat dry.

Heat a thin layer of olive oil in a skillet over medium-high heat. Fry eggplant slices until brown and crisp on both sides.

Mix tomato-basil sauce with eggplant and hot pasta.

VEAL RISOTTO
with Zucchini and Sage

4 servings

2 tbsp	PASTENE Pure Olive Oil	30 mL
1	small onion, chopped	1
1½ cups	PASTENE Italian Arborio Rice	375 mL
4 cups	veal or chicken stock, heated	1 liter
1 tbsp	PASTENE Pure Olive Oil	15 mL
¾ lb	veal tenderloin, cubed	400 g
2	medium zucchini, diced	2
½ cup	PASTENE Roasted Peppers, drained and cubed	125 mL
8	fresh sage leaves, minced	8
	salt and pepper	
	PASTENE Grated Parmesan Cheese	

- Heat olive oil in a heavy skillet over medium-high heat. Add onion and cook until soft. Add rice, stirring to coat all grains, and cook until lightly golden.

- Add 1 cup (250 mL) veal or chicken stock. Cook over medium heat until completely absorbed. Continue adding remaining stock one ladle at a time, stirring and cooking until liquid is absorbed between each addition. Cook about 18 minutes in total.

- Meanwhile, heat 1 tbsp (15 mL) olive oil in another skillet over medium-high heat. Cook veal for about 3 minutes or until browned on all sides.

- Stir veal into rice mixture, along with zucchini, roasted peppers, and sage. Cook over low heat 4-5 minutes, season to taste with salt and pepper, and serve immediately with Parmesan.

LINGUINE
with White Clam Sauce

3-4 servings

14 oz	**PASTENE Linguine**	400 g
¼ cup	**PASTENE Pure Olive Oil**	60 mL
3	garlic cloves, minced	3
1 tsp	fennel seeds	5 mL
½ cup	dry white wine	125 mL
2	cans (10.5 oz/142 g ea.) **PASTENE Baby Clams**	2
1½ cups	35% cream	375 mL
	salt and pepper	
	chopped fresh parsley	

- Cook linguine in boiling salted water until al dente. Drain and keep hot.
- Meanwhile, in a medium saucepan, heat olive oil over medium-high heat and cook garlic until soft, but not browned.
- Add fennel seeds, wine, and the clam juice from the clams. Season with salt and pepper. Bring to a boil for 2 minutes, then reduce heat, add cream and let simmer uncovered for 10 minutes.
- Add parsley and clams and cook until clams are heated. Serve with hot linguine.

PASTA
with Artichoke Hearts

4-6 servings

16 oz	PASTENE Tricolor Fusilli	500 g
4	jars (6½ fl. oz/170 mL ea.) PASTENE Marinated Artichokes Hearts	4
¼ tsp	crushed hot red peppers	1 mL
¾ cup	35% cream	175 mL
¼ cup	chopped fresh flat-leaf parsley	60 mL
2 tbsp	PASTENE Capers in Vinegar, drained	30 mL
1 cup	PASTENE Grated Parmesan Cheese	250 mL
	salt	

- Cook the pasta in boiling, salted water until al dente. Drain and keep hot.
- Meanwhile, drain the marinade from the artichokes into a large skillet. Add crushed hot pepper and salt to taste. Heat gently over low heat.
- Slice the artichoke hearts and add to skillet. Stir in cream. When heated, stir in the drained pasta, parsley, capers, and half the Parmesan.
- Serve in heated bowls topped with remaining Parmesan.

SPAGHETTINI
with Tomatoes and Mussels

4 servings

2 lbs	fresh mussels	1 kg
½ cup	dry white wine	125 mL
14 oz	PASTENE Spaghettini	400 g
4 tbsp	PASTENE Extra Virgin Olive Oil	60 mL
1	onion, chopped	1
1	can (28 fl. oz/796 mL) PASTENE Italian Peeled Tomatoes, chopped	1
2 tbsp	finely chopped fresh parsley	30 mL
	salt and pepper	
	PASTENE Grated Parmesan Cheese	

- Wash mussels and remove beards. Place in a large saucepan with the white wine. Cook over high heat, stirring constantly, until mussel shells open. Remove from heat. Discard any unopened mussels.

- Remove mussel meat from shells, and reserve meat and cooking liquid.

- Cook pasta in boiling salted water for 10 minutes; drain and reserve.

- Meanwhile, heat olive oil in a skillet over medium heat and add onion. Cook until onion is tender. Add tomatoes and reserved cooking liquid from mussels. Season to taste with salt and pepper. Cook over medium heat about 15 minutes.

- Add mussels. Cook over low heat a few minutes to reheat mussels, then mix with hot spaghettini; add parsley and serve hot, sprinkled with Parmesan.

FARFALLE
with Vegetables

4 servings

1 cup	PASTENE Sundried Tomatoes in Oil	250 mL
16 oz	PASTENE Farfalle	500 g
2 tbsp	PASTENE Extra Virgin Olive Oil	30 mL
2	garlic cloves, minced	2
1	onion, chopped	1
⅛ tsp	hot red pepper flakes (optional)	0.5 mL
1 cup	diced fresh green beans	250 mL
2	small zucchini, halved lengthwise and sliced	2
6	small pattypan squash, quartered	6
2	carrots, halved lengthwise and thinly sliced	2
1 cup	chicken stock	250 mL
½ cup	PASTENE Grated Parmesan Cheese	125 mL
¼ cup	chopped fresh parsley	60 mL
8	fresh basil leaves	8

- Drain sundried tomatoes and cut in half. Set aside.
- Cook pasta in boiling salted water for 10 minutes; drain and keep hot.
- Meanwhile, heat olive oil in a skillet over medium-high heat. Add garlic, onion and red pepper flakes (optional). Cook 2 minutes. Add green beans, zucchini, squash and carrots. Stir-fry until tender-crisp, about 5 minutes.
- Add chicken stock and simmer 1 minute. In a large bowl, toss together vegetable mixture with hot pasta, Parmesan, sundried tomatoes, parsley and basil. Mix well and serve immediately, with more Parmesan if desired.

SEAFOOD
Risotto

4-6 servings

4 tbsp	PASTENE Extra Virgin Olive Oil	60 mL
1½ cups	PASTENE Italian Arborio Rice	375 mL
2	garlic cloves, minced	2
3 cups	fish or chicken stock	750 mL
1	can (10.5 oz/142 g) PASTENE Baby Clams	1
1	pinch of saffron	1
12	fresh shrimps, peeled and deveined	12
12	fresh scallops	12
1 tbsp	chopped fresh parsley	15 mL
1 tbsp	chopped fresh basil	15 mL
	PASTENE Grated Parmesan Cheese	

- Heat olive oil in a saucepan over medium heat. Add rice and garlic. Cook until lightly browned.

- Add 1 cup (250 mL) fish or chicken stock. Continue cooking, stirring, until liquid is absorbed. Add remaining stock one ladle at a time until absorbed.

- Add clam juice from clams (reserve clams for later) and saffron. Mix well. Cook until rice is nearly tender. Arrange shrimps and scallops on top of rice, cover, and cook 5 minutes until seafood is cooked.

- Stir in parsley, basil, and reserved clams. Serve hot with grated Parmesan, if desired.

SAVORY BLACK BEANS
with Rapini

6 servings

2	cans (14 fl. oz/398 mL each) PASTENE Black Beans	2
3 tbsp	PASTENE Pure Olive Oil	45 mL
1	medium onion, chopped	1
½ cup	chopped celery	125 mL
1	jar (7 fl. oz/170 mL) PASTENE Roasted Peppers, diced	1
2 cups	chopped rapini	500 mL
1 tsp	chopped fresh oregano	5 mL
1 tbsp	PASTENE Balsamic Vinegar	15 mL
	salt and pepper	

- Rinse and drain black beans.
- Heat oil in a saucepan over medium-high heat. Cook onion and celery for about 5 minutes. Add roasted peppers and rapini and cook about 5 minutes.
- Stir in black beans, oregano, balsamic vinegar, and salt and pepper to taste. Cook until heated through and serve hot as a side dish.

GNOCCHI
with Tomato Sauce

4 servings

1½ lbs	potatoes, peeled and cut in pieces	750 g
1½ cups	flour	375 mL
2	egg yolks, beaten	2
¼ cup	PASTENE Grated Parmesan Cheese	60 mL
	pinch of nutmeg	
	salt and pepper	
	tomato sauce (see recipe below)	
	PASTENE Grated Parmesan Cheese	

- Boil potatoes in salted water until tender. Drain well and continue cooking 2 minutes, until dry. Mash potatoes with a fork.
- Add most of the flour, egg yolks, Parmesan cheese, and nutmeg. Mix to a smooth dough. Add more flour if necessary to make a dough that does not stick to your hands.
- Place dough on a floured surface. Cut into 4 pieces, and roll each into a long rope about ½ inch (1 cm) in diameter. Cut each rope into 1 inch (2.5 cm) lengths. Flatten each piece gently with a fork or fingertip.
- Drop pieces of dough, a few at a time, into boiling salted water. As soon as they rise to the surface, remove them with a slotted spoon, drain well and keep hot until all gnocchi are cooked. Serve with tomato sauce and grated Parmesan.

PASTENE
Tomato Sauce

4 servings

4 tbsp	PASTENE Pure Olive Oil	60 mL
3	garlic cloves, chopped	3
1	can (28 fl. oz/796 mL) PASTENE Diced Ready Spiced Tomatoes, or PASTENE Chunky "Kitchen Ready" Ground Tomatoes	1
1 tbsp	chopped fresh oregano	15 mL
6-8	fresh basil leaves	6-8
	salt and freshly ground black pepper	

- Heat olive oil in a large skillet over medium heat. Cook the garlic until soft, but not browned.
- Increase the heat to high and add tomatoes. Add salt and pepper to taste. Cook 5 to 7 minutes, stirring frequently. Remove from heat and stir in the oregano and basil. Serve with gnocchi or pasta.

RED TUNA SAUCE
with Farfalle

4-6 servings

16 oz	PASTENE Farfalle pasta	500 g
3 tbsp	PASTENE Extra Virgin Olive Oil	45 mL
4	garlic cloves, sliced	4
½	onion, chopped	½
½ cup	PASTENE Sun-Dried Tomatoes in Oil, drained and chopped	125 mL
½ cup	PASTENE Capers in Vinegar, drained	125 mL
¼ tsp	dried red pepper flakes	1 mL
1½ cups	chicken stock	375 mL
1	can (28 fl. oz/796 mL) PASTENE Chunky "Kitchen Ready" Ground Tomatoes	1
4 tbsp	PASTENE Balsamic Vinegar	60 mL
1½ tbsp	chopped fresh flat-leaf parsley	20 mL
2	cans (6 oz/198 g ea.) PASTENE Light Meat Tuna (Tonno), drained	2
3 tbsp	chopped fresh basil	45 mL
	salt and pepper	
	PASTENE Grated Parmesan Cheese	

- Cook farfalle in boiling salted water until al dente; drain and keep hot.
- Meanwhile, heat olive oil in a large skillet over medium-high heat. Cook garlic and onion until soft. Add sundried tomatoes, capers, and red pepper flakes. Stir in chicken stock, tomatoes, vinegar, parsley, and salt and pepper to taste. Bring to a boil, then reduce heat and let simmer for 10 minutes.
- Stir in the tuna and basil and heat through. Mix sauce with hot pasta and serve immediately with Parmesan.

Heat olive oil in a large skillet over medium-high heat. Cook garlic and onion until soft. Add sundried tomatoes, capers, and red pepper flakes.

Stir in chicken stock, tomatoes, vinegar, parsley, and salt and pepper to taste. Bring to a boil, then reduce heat and let simmer for 10 minutes.

Stir in the tuna and basil and heat through.

PENNE
Puttanesca

4 servings

5	garlic cloves, chopped	5
2 tbsp	PASTENE Extra Virgin Olive Oil	30 mL
1	jar (10 fl. oz/295 mL) PASTENE Calamata Olives, drained	1
1	can (28 fl. oz/796 mL) PASTENE "Kitchen Ready" Ground Tomatoes	1
½	can (2 oz/48 g) PASTENE Anchovy Fillets in Olive Oil, finely chopped	½
½ cup	PASTENE Capers in Vinegar, drained	125 mL
⅓ cup	chopped fresh parsley	75 mL
16 oz	PASTENE Penne pasta	500 g
	salt and pepper	

- In a large skillet, heat the garlic in the olive oil. Add the olives, tomatoes, anchovies, capers, parsley, salt and pepper. Bring to a boil, reduce heat and simmer uncovered for 30 minutes.
- Cook penne in boiling salted water until al dente. Drain and serve immediately with sauce.

PESTO BASIL
Rice

4 servings

4	slices of prosciutto ham, cut in 4 pieces	4
2 tbsp	PASTENE Pure Olive Oil	30 mL
3	dry shallots, chopped	3
1	garlic clove, finely chopped	1
3 cups	chicken stock	750 mL
1 cup	PASTENE Italian Arborio Rice	250 mL
¼ cup	dry white wine	60 mL
¼ cup	PASTENE Pesto Basil Sauce	60 mL
	PASTENE Grated Parmesan Cheese	
	fresh basil leaves	

- Preheat oven to 350°F (180°C).
- Arrange prosciutto on a baking sheet and bake in oven about 7 minutes. Set aside.
- Heat olive oil in a large saucepan over medium heat, and cook shallots and garlic until soft. Meanwhile, in a second saucepan, heat the broth to simmering.
- When shallots and garlic are soft, stir in the rice to coat thoroughly with oil. Stir in the wine until it is absorbed.
- Start ladling in the heated stock, ½ cup (125 mL) at a time, stirring until it is almost completely absorbed before adding the next ladleful. Add pesto sauce.
- After about 13 minutes, start tasting the rice. It is properly cooked when the rice grains are no longer crunchy when bitten. Add a bit more hot liquid if necessary, remove rice from heat and serve as soon as it is tender.
- Serve garnished with Parmesan, prosciutto crisps, and fresh basil.

PESTO FETTUCINE
with Chicken and Anchovies

4 servings

16 oz	PASTENE Fettuccine	500 g
2 tbsp	PASTENE Extra Virgin Olive Oil	30 mL
1 lb	boneless chicken, in strips	500 g
2	onions, halved and sliced	2
2	garlic cloves, minced	2
1	can (28 fl. oz/796 mL) PASTENE Diced Ready Spiced Tomatoes	1
1 tbsp	chopped fresh oregano	15 mL
6	PASTENE Anchovy Fillets in Oil, drained and chopped	6
1	pinch of sugar	1
1	jar (7 fl. oz/170 mL) PASTENE Roasted Peppers, sliced	1
2 tbsp	PASTENE Pesto Basil Sauce	30 mL
2 cups	fresh spinach, washed and trimmed	500 mL
½ cup	PASTENE Grated Parmesan Cheese	125 mL
	salt and pepper	

- Cook pasta in boiling salted water for 10 minutes or until al dente; drain and keep hot.
- Meanwhile, heat half the oil in a saucepan over medium-high heat. Add chicken and cook, stirring, until browned, about 5 minutes. Season with salt and pepper; remove from saucepan and set aside.
- In the same saucepan, add remaining oil and cook onions and garlic for about 5 minutes. Add tomatoes, oregano, anchovies, and sugar. Cook for 5 minutes.
- Stir in roasted peppers, pesto sauce, spinach, and chicken. Simmer 3 minutes until spinach is tender, add fettucine and Parmesan; mix well. Serve immediately.

Main Courses

These days, our taste buds are far
more adventurous than in the past.
We're no longer satisified with plain
old meat and potatoes every day.
We want lively flavors, interesting food
combinations, and healthy dishes that
taste richly satisfying without the
addition of lots of butter, cream or
heavy sauces.

The recipes in this chapter have been
selected to provide you with an
interesting cross-section of updated
classics and the very latest
international flavors. And you'll find
that with a selection of convenient and
flavor-packed Pastene products on
hand, they are as easy to make as they
are delicious!

OSSO
Buco

4 servings

8	veal shanks, 1 in. (2.5 cm) thick	8
1 cup	all-purpose flour	250 mL
3 tbsp	PASTENE Extra Virgin Olive Oil	45 mL
1	onion, chopped	1
1	carrot, finely diced	1
1	celery stalk, finely diced	1
2	garlic cloves, chopped	2
½ tsp	dried basil	2 mL
¼ tsp	dried thyme	1 mL
2	bay leaves	2
2½ tbsp	chopped fresh parsley	35 mL
1 cup	dry white wine	250 mL
1 can	(28 fl. oz/796 mL) PASTENE Diced Ready Spiced Tomatoes	1
1⅔ cups	PASTENE "Kitchen Ready" Ground Tomatoes	400 mL
1 cup	veal or chicken stock, heated	250 mL
	salt and pepper	

- Preheat oven to 350°F (180°C).
- Season veal shanks with salt and pepper and coat lightly with flour.
- In a large casserole, heat olive oil over medium heat. Add half the veal and brown 5 minutes on each side. Remove and repeat for remaining veal. Remove from casserole and set aside.
- Add onion, carrot, celery, garlic, basil, thyme, bay leaves and parsley to casserole. Cook 2 minutes at medium-high heat. Pour in wine and continue cooking for 4 minutes.
- Return veal shanks to casserole and add remaining ingredients. Cook in oven at least 1½ hours, covered, or until veal is very tender.
- Serve immediately, garnished with Basil Gremolata (see below).

BASIL GREMOLATA

- In a bowl, combine the grated zest of 1 orange and 1 lemon with ¼ cup (60 mL) chopped fresh basil. Sprinkle over cooked Osso Buco.

LAMB CHOPS PARMESAN
with Black Olives

4 servings

8	lamb chops	8
1½ cups	PASTENE Grated Parmesan Cheese	375 mL
2 cups	PASTENE Flavored Bread Crumbs	500 mL
2	eggs, beaten	2
3 tbsp	PASTENE Extra Virgin Olive Oil	45 mL
1 cup	PASTENE Pitted Olives, sliced	250 mL
	2 lemons, sliced, for garnish	
	salt and pepper	
	PASTENE Pasta of your choice	

- Preheat oven to 350°F (180°C).
- Trim excess fat from lamb and season with salt and pepper.
- Put Parmesan in a bowl, and breadcrumbs in a second bowl.
- Dip lamb chops on both sides first in Parmesan, then in beaten eggs and finally in breadcrumbs.
- In an ovenproof skillet, heat olive oil over medium-high heat and cook chops for 2 minutes on each side. Add black olives to skillet.
- Bake in preheated oven for 7 minutes or until chops are cooked to taste. Serve immediately with lemon slices and hot, cooked pasta.

TURBOT FILLETS
Poached in Wine

4 servings

1 tbsp	**PASTENE Pure Olive Oil**	15 mL
½ cup	**dry white wine**	125 mL
1 cup	**fish stock**	250 mL
2	**dry shallots, thinly sliced**	2
4	**large turbot fillets**	4
2 tbsp	**PASTENE Capers in Vinegar, drained**	30 mL
2 tbsp	**PASTENE Pesto Basil Sauce**	30 mL
¼ cup	**35% cream**	60 mL
	salt and pepper	

• Combine olive oil, white wine, and fish stock in a skillet. Add shallots, salt and pepper. Cover, bring to a boil and cook 2 minutes over high heat.

• Lower heat so liquid is no longer bubbling. Arrange fillets in skillet and cook 2 minutes. Carefully turn fillets with spatula and cook another 2 minutes. Remove fillets from pan and set aside.

• Add capers, pesto, and cream to cooking liquid. Cook 3 to 4 minutes over high heat or until sauce thickens. Season to taste with salt and pepper and pour over fish to serve.

PROSCIUTTO-STUFFED
Veal Cutlets

4 servings

4	large veal cutlets, flattened	4
4	slices of prosciutto ham	4
1 cup	PASTENE Grated Romano Cheese	250 mL
2 tbsp	PASTENE Extra Virgin Olive Oil	30 mL
2	dry shallots, finely chopped	2
1	celery stalk, finely diced	1
½ lb	fresh mushrooms, cleaned and quartered	250 g
2 tbsp	PASTENE Pesto Basil Sauce	30 mL
1 cup	chicken stock, heated	250 mL
	freshly ground pepper	
	salt and pepper	
	Pastene Linguine	

- Preheat oven to 350°F (180°C).

- Spread veal cutlets flat on cutting board, season with freshly ground pepper, and top each with a slice of prosciutto. Sprinkle with cheese and roll; tie each roll closed with kitchen string.

- Heat oil in large skillet over medium heat. Add veal rolls and sear 5 minutes, browning on all sides. Remove from pan to a baking dish and cook in oven 7 to 10 minutes.

- Meanwhile, add shallots and celery to skillet. Cook 4 minutes. Add mushrooms, season to taste with salt and pepper, and cook 3 minutes over high heat.

- Stir in pesto and chicken stock. Cook over medium heat for 5 minutes. Slice veal rolls crosswise and serve with sauce and hot cooked Pastene linguine.

CLASSIC MUSSELS
Marinara

4-6 servings

4 lbs	fresh mussels	2 kg
4 tbsp	PASTENE Extra Virgin Olive Oil	60 mL
1	onion, chopped	1
3	garlic cloves, chopped	3
⅓ cup	dry white wine	75 mL
1 tsp	chopped fresh oregano	5 mL
¼ tsp	dried crushed chili peppers	1 mL
2 cups	PASTENE "Kitchen Ready" Ground Tomatoes	500 mL
2 tbsp	PASTENE Pesto Basil Sauce	30 mL
4 tbsp	chopped fresh parsley	60 mL
	salt and pepper	
	PASTENE Grated Parmesan Cheese	

- Rinse mussels in cold water, and remove beards. Discard any mussels that do not close when shells are tapped.
- Heat olive oil in a large pot over medium heat. Cook onion until soft, but not browned. Add garlic and wine. Cook for 5 minutes over medium-high heat.
- Add oregano and chili pepper. Cook another 5 minutes. Add mussels, cover, and cook 10 minutes, or until mussels open.
- Remove mussels with a slotted spoon and keep hot. Discard any unopened mussels. Add tomatoes to pan. Simmer 8 minutes. Stir in pesto sauce, parsley and reserved mussels. Season to taste with salt and pepper. Mix well and serve immediately, sprinkled with Parmesan if desired.

Rinse mussels in cold water, and remove beards. Discard any mussels that do not close when shells are tapped.

Heat olive oil in a large pot over medium heat. Cook onion until soft. Add garlic and wine. Cook for 5 minutes over medium-high heat.

Add oregano and chili pepper. Cook another 5 minutes. Add mussels, cover, and cook 10 minutes, or until mussels open.

Remove mussels with a slotted spoon and keep hot. Discard any unopened mussels. Add tomatoes.

Simmer 8 minutes, then stir in pesto sauce and parsley.

Add reserved mussels and season to taste with salt and pepper. Mix well.

WHITE FISH
with Tomato Sauce

4 servings

5 tbsp	PASTENE Extra Virgin Olive Oil	75 mL
4	garlic cloves, minced	4
1 tbsp	finely chopped parsley	15 mL
4	pieces of white fish	4
4 tbsp	PASTENE Extra Virgin Olive Oil	60 mL
	juice of ½ lemon	
	tomato sauce (see recipe on page 118)	

- In a bowl, combine 5 tbsp (75 mL) of olive oil with garlic, parsley and lemon juice.
- Wash fish and pat dry with paper towels. Place in lemon juice mixture, making sure all fish is coated. Refrigerate at least 1 hour.
- Heat 4 tbsp (60 mL) of oil in a skillet over medium heat and add fish (discard marinade). Cook until golden on both sides, turning once. Remove from skillet and serve topped with tomato sauce.

HALIBUT
with Saffron and Tomatoes

4 servings

1	pinch of saffron threads	1
1¼ lbs	halibut steaks	575 g
2 tbsp	all-purpose flour	30 mL
2 tbsp	PASTENE Pure Olive Oil	30 mL
1	red pepper, sliced	1
1	yellow pepper, sliced	1
1	onion, finely chopped	1
1	garlic clove, chopped	1
1	can (28 fl. oz/796 mL) PASTENE Italian Peeled Tomatoes, drained and chopped	1
1 tbsp	finely chopped parsley	15 mL
	salt and pepper	

- Preheat oven to 350°F (180°C). Soak saffron in a little hot water.
- Sprinkle halibut with flour on both sides. Heat oil in a skillet and cook fish, at medium heat, until browned on both sides.
- Season to taste with salt and pepper and transfer fish to baking pan. Bake 8-10 minutes, or until cooked through.
- Meanwhile, add peppers, onion and garlic to skillet. Cook until tender-crisp. Add tomatoes and parsley. Cook 3-4 minutes. Stir in saffron with its soaking liquid and simmer 10 minutes. Season to taste with salt and pepper and serve with halibut.

RAGOUT OF PORK
with Eggplant

4 servings

2 tbsp	PASTENE Extra Virgin Olive Oil	30 mL
1 lb	lean, boneless pork, cubed	500 g
2	onions, sliced	2
1	can (28 fl. oz/796 mL) PASTENE Diced Ready Spiced Tomatoes	1
2 cups	cubed peeled eggplant	500 mL
1 cup	PASTENE Pitted Olives, sliced	250 mL
	salt and pepper	

- Preheat oven to 350°F (180°C).
- Heat olive oil in a skillet over medium-high heat. Add pork and brown on all sides. Add onions and cook for 4 minutes. Season to taste with salt and pepper.
- Transfer mixture to a casserole or baking dish with a cover. Stir in tomatoes and eggplant. Bake in oven about 1 hour.
- Stir in black olives. Bake another 15 minutes and serve immediately. Swiss chard makes a nice accompaniment.

GARLIC CHICKEN
Drumsticks

4 servings

2 lbs	chicken drumsticks	1 kg
2 tsp	PASTENE Pure Olive Oil	10 mL
¾ cup	PASTENE Flavored Bread Crumbs	175 mL
1 tsp	garlic powder	5 mL
	salt and pepper	

- Preheat oven to 350°F (180°C).
- Skin chicken and remove visible fat; brush with olive oil.
- In a bowl, mix breadcrumbs, garlic powder, and salt and pepper to taste. Coat chicken with breadcrumb mixture and place in a single layer on baking pan.
- Cook in oven for 35 to 40 minutes, turning once or twice to brown all sides. Serve hot.

CLASSIC BEEF AND TOMATO
Stew

4-6 servings

6	potatoes, peeled and cubed	6
2 tbsp	PASTENE Pure Olive Oil	30 mL
1	medium onion, chopped	1
2 lb	diced boneless beef	1 kg
1	can (28 fl. oz/796 mL) PASTENE "Kitchen Ready" Ground Tomatoes	1
	salt and pepper	

- Preheat oven to 350°F (180°C).
- In a baking dish, coat potatoes with olive oil. Add onion and diced beef. Mix well and bake for about 30 minutes.
- Add tomatoes and mix well. Add salt and pepper to taste; return to oven to cook for another 30 minutes, or until beef is tender.
- Serve with cooked PASTENE Italian Arborio Rice, if desired.

LAMB
with Sundried Tomatoes

4 servings

2 tbsp	PASTENE Extra Virgin Olive Oil	30 mL
4	slices of leg of lamb	4
1 tbsp	chopped fresh rosemary	15 mL
1	onion, chopped	1
1	zucchini, chopped	1
½ cup	PASTENE Sundried Tomatoes in Oil, drained and chopped	125 mL
	PASTENE Spaghetti, cooked and still hot	
	salt and pepper	

- Preheat oven to 375°F (190°C).
- Heat oil in a skillet over medium heat and brown lamb on both sides. Sprinkle with rosemary. Place in baking dish and bake in oven 6-7 minutes or until done to taste.
- Meanwhile, in same skillet, cook onion and zucchini for 5 minutes. Add sundried tomatoes, and salt and pepper to taste. Cook for 5 minutes.
- Serve lamb and vegetables with cooked spaghetti.

ROAST ROUND OF BEEF
with Artichokes

4 servings

1 tbsp	PASTENE Pure Olive Oil	15 mL
3 lb	beef round roast	1.4 kg
1	red onion, finely chopped	1
1	celery stalk, finely chopped	1
2	garlic cloves, chopped	2
1 tsp	chopped fresh thyme	5 mL
1 tsp	chopped fresh oregano	5 mL
1½ cups	beef stock, heated	375 mL
½ cup	PASTENE "Kitchen Ready" Ground Tomatoes	125 mL
3 tbsp	PASTENE Tomato Paste	45 mL
1 tbsp	PASTENE Pesto Basil Sauce	15 mL
	PASTENE Artichoke Hearts, drained and heated in oil	
	salt and pepper	

- Preheat oven to 425°F (220°C).
- Heat olive oil in a roasting pan over medium-high heat and brown beef on all sides. Season with salt and pepper.
- Place pan in oven and roast for about 15 minutes, then reduce heat to 375°F (190°C) and add onion, celery, garlic, thyme and oregano. Continue cooking 35 to 40 minutes.
- When beef is tender, remove pan from oven; set beef aside to keep warm. Place roasting pan with its drippings on stovetop over high heat. Add beef stock, tomatoes, tomato paste, and pesto sauce. Cook, stirring, for 5 minutes. Season with salt and pepper to taste.
- Serve sauce with sliced beef and artichoke hearts sautéed in a little olive oil.

CHILI
con Carne

4 servings

1 tbsp	**PASTENE Pure Olive Oil**	15 mL
1	**large onion, diced**	1
1 tbsp	**chili powder**	15 mL
1 tbsp	**ground cumin**	15 mL
1 tsp	**mustard powder**	5 mL
1 lb	**lean ground beef**	500 g
2	**cans (28 fl. oz/796 mL ea.) PASTENE Italian Peeled Tomatoes, chopped**	2
2 tbsp	**PASTENE Tomato Paste**	30 mL
2	**cans (14 fl. oz/398 mL ea.) PASTENE Red Kidney Beans, drained and rinsed**	2
1 cup	**PASTENE Pitted Ripe Black Olives**	250 mL
2 tbsp	**chopped fresh coriander salt and pepper**	30 mL

- Heat olive oil in a large saucepan over medium heat. Add onion and cook 2 minutes, then stir in chili powder, cumin, mustard and ground beef. Cook, stirring, until beef is browned.
- Add tomatoes and tomato paste. Cook 45 minutes over low heat.
- Stir in kidney beans and olives. Season to taste. Simmer 5 minutes and serve sprinkled with coriander. Suggested side dish: tortilla chips or vegetable rice.

VEAL SCALLOPINE
Saltimbocca

6-8 servings

8	veal scallopine (boneless cutlets)	8
8	slices of prosciutto ham	8
8	fresh sage leaves	8
½ cup	all-purpose flour	125 mL
3 tbsp	PASTENE Pure Olive Oil	45 mL
½ cup	dry white wine	125 mL
1 tbsp	PASTENE Tomato Paste	15 mL
1	envelope of demi-glace or brown gravy mix	1
⅓ cup	PASTENE Pitted Olives, sliced	75 mL

- Lay veal slices flat, and lay a slice of prosciutto on each. Top with a sage leaf, and secure with a toothpick.
- Coat each piece of veal lightly in flour.
- Heat olive oil in a skillet over medium-high heat. Cook veal about 2 minutes on each side. Remove from pan and keep hot.
- Add wine to skillet. Stir and bring to a boil. Stir in tomato paste and demi-glace or gravy mix (dissolved according to package directions). Stir in olive slices and heat through. Serve veal with olive sauce, and vegetables of your choice.

Lay veal slices flat, and lay a slice of prosciutto on each.

Top with a sage leaf, and secure with a toothpick.

Coat each piece of veal lightly in flour.

Heat olive oil in a skillet over medium-high heat. Cook veal about 2 minutes on each side. Remove from pan and keep hot.

Add wine to skillet. Stir and bring to a boil. Stir in tomato paste and demi-glace or gravy mix (dissolved according to package directions).

Stir in olive slices and heat through.

BARBECUED PORK CHOPS
with Artichokes

4 servings

1	jar (6 fl. oz/170 mL) PASTENE Marinated Artichoke Hearts	1
1 tsp	Tabasco sauce	5 mL
4	boneless pork chops, fat trimmed	4
1½ cups	PASTENE Diced Ready Spiced Tomatoes	375 mL
½ cup	PASTENE Roasted Peppers, drained and chopped	125 mL
¼ cup	PASTENE Pitted Olives, sliced	60 mL
	salt and pepper	

- Drain artichoke hearts, reserving liquid in a separate bowl. Combine artichoke liquid with Tabasco. Add pork chops, coat with Tabasco mixture, and let marinate in refrigerator for at least 30 minutes.

- In a second bowl, combine artichoke hearts, tomatoes, red peppers and black olives. Season with salt and pepper. Set aside.

- When ready to cook, drain pork chops and discard marinade. Cook chops on preheated barbecue at medium heat for 3-5 minutes on each side, or until done to taste.

- Serve immediately with artichoke mixture and greens of your choice.

PORK TENDERLOIN
Carbonade

4 servings

3 tbsp	PASTENE Extra Virgin Olive Oil	45 mL
2	pork tenderloins, trimmed of fat	2
1	red onion, finely chopped	1
1	celery stalk, finely chopped	1
1	garlic clove, chopped	1
1 tsp	dried oregano	5 mL
1 cup	beer	250 mL
1	can (28 fl. oz/796 mL) PASTENE Diced Ready Spiced Tomatoes	1
3 tbsp	PASTENE Tomato Paste	45 mL
	salt and pepper	

- Heat olive oil in a skillet over medium heat. Add pork and cook 5 minutes until browned on all sides. Season with salt and pepper.

- Add onion, celery, garlic, and oregano and cook 5 minutes. Pour in beer and cook 2 minutes over medium-high heat.

- Add tomatoes and tomato paste and continue cooking for 10 minutes over medium heat.

- Remove pork from skillet and continue cooking sauce for 3 minutes over high heat. Season to taste with salt and pepper. Serve sauce over sliced pork.

SWISS
Steak

4 servings

3 tbsp	PASTENE Pure Olive Oil	45 mL
1	red onion, thinly sliced	1
1	green pepper, thinly sliced	1
2 cups	PASTENE Italian Peeled Tomatoes, drained and chopped	500 mL
1 tsp	dried oregano	5 mL
1 lb	boneless steak, trimmed of fat and thinly sliced	500 g
	salt and pepper	
	hot pepper sauce	
	PASTENE Italian Arborio Rice	

- Heat 2 tbsp (30 mL) of the oil in a skillet over medium heat. Add onion and pepper; cook 4 minutes.

- Stir in tomatoes, oregano and a few drops of hot pepper sauce; season well. Cook 12 minutes over medium heat.

- Meanwhile, heat remaining oil in a second skillet over medium-high heat. When hot, add half the meat and cook 1 minute on each side over high heat; season well with salt and pepper. Set aside. Repeat for remaining meat.

- Add cooked meat to skillet with tomato mixture and simmer 1 minute. Serve with hot, cooked rice.

148

SCAMPI
with Herb and Balsamic Sauce

4 servings

1	red onion, finely chopped	1
½ cup	PASTENE Extra Virgin Olive Oil	125 mL
1 tsp	chopped fresh rosemary	5 mL
2 tsp	chopped fresh basil	10 mL
1 tbsp	PASTENE Balsamic Vinegar	15 mL
¼ tsp	black pepper	1 mL
1 lb	raw medium scampi, shelled and deveined	500 g
1	leek, white part only, in julienne strips	1
8	small pattypan squash	8
	PASTENE Grated Parmesan Cheese	
	salt and pepper	

- Combine onion, ½ cup (125 mL) olive oil, rosemary, basil, vinegar and pepper. Pour mixture over scampi. Toss to coat and let marinate 30 minutes.

- Meanwhile, cook julienned leek in boiling salted water 2 minutes. Drain and reserve.

- Cook pattypan squash in boiling salted water for 8 minutes. Drain, quarter and set aside.

- Heat scampi marinade in a skillet over medium-high heat. Add scampi and cook about 5 minutes, turning once.

- Season leek and squash with salt and pepper. Serve with scampi and some of the hot marinade sauce, garnished with grated Parmesan shavings.

CHICKEN BREASTS
with Capers and Sundried Tomatoes

4 servings

1 tbsp	PASTENE Extra Virgin Olive Oil	15 mL
4	skinless, boneless chicken breast halves	4
6	PASTENE Sundried Tomatoes in Oil, drained and chopped	6
1½ cups	chicken stock, heated	375 mL
1 tbsp	PASTENE Tomato Paste	15 mL
¼ cup	PASTENE Capers in Vinegar, drained	60 mL
	salt and pepper	

- Preheat oven to 350°F (180°C).
- Heat oil in a skillet over medium heat. Add chicken, and brown 4-5 minutes on each side. Season to taste with salt and pepper.
- Remove chicken to a baking dish and cook in oven for 12-15 minutes, or until chicken is no longer pink inside.
- Using same skillet, stir in sundried tomatoes, chicken stock, tomato paste and capers. Mix well and season to taste with salt and pepper. Keep hot until ready to serve.
- Slice chicken and top with sundried tomato sauce. Serve with risotto, if desired.

Heat oil in a skillet over medium heat. Add chicken, and brown 4-5 minutes on each side. Season to taste with salt and pepper.

Remove chicken to a baking dish and cook in oven for 12-15 minutes, or until chicken is no longer pink inside.

Using same skillet, stir in sundried tomatoes, chicken stock, tomato paste and capers. Mix well and season to taste with salt and pepper.

ROAST LOIN OF PORK
Italian Style

4 servings

1 tbsp	PASTENE Extra Virgin Olive Oil	15 mL
2 tbsp	PASTENE Pesto Basil Sauce	30 mL
2	garlic cloves, chopped	2
3 lb	pork loin, tied	1.4 kg
1	onion, finely chopped	1
1	celery stalk, finely chopped	1
1 tsp	parsley, finely chopped	5 mL
1 cup	beef stock, heated	250 mL
1½ cups	PASTENE Diced Ready Spiced Tomatoes	375 mL
2 tbsp	PASTENE Tomato Paste	30 mL
1 tsp	cornstarch	5 mL
2 tbsp	cold water	30 mL
	juice of ½ lemon	
	salt and pepper	

- Preheat oven to 400°F (200°C).
- Combine oil, pesto sauce, garlic, and lemon juice. Place pork loin in a roasting pan and brush with the pesto mixture. Roast in oven 20 minutes.
- Sprinkle meat with salt and pepper. Add onion, celery and parsley to roasting pan; cook another 35 minutes or until meat is cooked to taste.
- Remove pork loin from pan and reserve. Set roasting pan on stovetop over high heat. Pour in beef stock, tomatoes, and tomato paste. Season to taste with salt and pepper. Cook, stirring, for 6 minutes.
- Dissolve cornstarch in the water; stir into tomato sauce and cook another 2 minutes or until thickened. Serve sliced pork loin with sauce.

SALMON TROUT
with Black Olives

4 servings

2 tbsp	PASTENE Extra Virgin Olive Oil	30 mL
4	salmon trout fillets, 5 oz (150 g) each	4
2	PASTENE Hearts of Palm, sliced thick	2
1	jar (6 fl. oz/170 mL) PASTENE Marinated Artichoke Hearts, drained	1
1	can (15 oz) PASTENE Broken Straw Mushrooms, drained and sliced, or 20 fresh mushrooms, cleaned and sliced	1
1 tsp	grated lemon zest	5 mL
12	PASTENE Pitted Black Olives	12
1 tbsp	chopped fresh parsley	15 mL
	juice of 1 lemon	
	salt and pepper	

- Heat olive oil in a skillet over medium heat. Season fish with salt and pepper to taste. Place in skillet skin-side down. Cook 2 minutes. Turn filets over; cook 2 more minutes or until done to taste. Remove fish to serving platter and keep hot.

- Add hearts of palm, artichoke hearts, mushrooms, lemon zest and olives to the same pan; cook 4 minutes over medium heat. Season well, sprinkle with parsley and lemon juice. Mix and pour over fish. Serve immediately.

SAUTÉED CHICKEN LIVERS
with Olives

4 servings

3 tbsp	PASTENE Extra Virgin Olive Oil	45 mL
1 lb	chicken livers, trimmed of fat and halved	500 g
1	red onion, chopped	1
1	celery stalk, finely diced	1
1 tsp	dried oregano	5 mL
2 cups	chicken stock, heated	500 mL
2 tbsp	PASTENE Tomato Paste	30 mL
1 tbsp	cornstarch	15 mL
3 tbsp	cold water	45 mL
⅓ cup	PASTENE Pitted Olives, sliced	75 mL
⅓ cup	PASTENE Roasted Peppers, diced	75 mL
	chopped fresh parsley	
	salt and pepper	

- In a skillet, heat 2 tbsp (30 mL) olive oil over medium heat. Season chicken livers with salt and pepper. Add half of the livers to pan; cook 3 minutes. Remove cooked livers and cook second batch 3 minutes. Set livers aside.

- Add remaining oil to pan. Add onion, celery and oregano; season to taste with salt and pepper. Cook 5 minutes over high heat.

- Stir in chicken stock and tomato paste; cook 3 minutes over medium heat. Dissolve cornstarch in the cold water; stir into skillet. Cook 1 minute.

- Return livers to skillet, add olives and roasted peppers; stir well and simmer for 4 minutes over low heat. Sprinkle with parsley and serve immediately.

PARMESAN VEAL CHOPS
with Tomato

4 servings

2 tbsp	all-purpose flour	30 mL
1	egg, lightly beaten	1
½ cup	PASTENE Flavored Bread Crumbs	125 mL
⅓ cup	PASTENE Grated Parmesan Cheese	75 mL
4	veal chops	4
2 tbsp	PASTENE Pure Olive Oil	30 mL
2	onions, sliced	2
1	can (28 fl. oz/796 mL) PASTENE Diced Ready Spiced Tomatoes	1
	salt and pepper	
	fresh parsley, chopped	

- Preheat oven to 300°F (150°C).
- Place flour in a bowl, beaten egg in a second bowl. In a third bowl, combine breadcrumbs and cheese.
- Dip veal chops first in flour, then in egg and finally in breadcrumb-cheese mixture.
- Heat 1 tbsp (15 mL) olive oil in a skillet over medium-high heat. Add veal chops and brown on both sides; remove chops and bake in preheated oven about 10 minutes or until done to taste.
- Meanwhile, heat remaining olive oil in a medium saucepan over medium heat. Add onions and cook about 5 minutes, stirring occasionally. Add tomatoes, season to taste with salt and pepper, and cook uncovered for 7-8 minutes. Serve chops with tomato sauce mixture, garnished with parsley if desired.

SPICED PORK
Kebabs

4-6 servings

2 lbs	cubed boneless pork tenderloin	1 kg
1 cup	PASTENE Flavored Bread Crumbs	250 mL
½ tsp	dry mustard	2 mL
1 tsp	mixed dried herbs of your choice	5 mL
1	egg, beaten	1
8-12	bamboo skewers, soaked in water 10 minutes	8-12
	PASTENE Italian Arborio Rice	
	dash of salt	

- Thread 5 to 6 cubes of pork on each wooden skewer.
- Combine breadcrumbs, dry mustard, herbs, and salt in a bowl.
- In a separate bowl, put beaten egg. Dip skewered pork in breadcrumb mixture, then in beaten egg, and again in breadcrumbs.
- Bake pork kebabs in oven at 350°F (180°C) for about 35 to 40 minutes. Serve with vegetables and rice.

PORK AND VEGETABLE
Stir-fry

4 servings

1 tbsp	PASTENE Pure Olive Oil	15 mL
1	pork tenderloin, trimmed of fat and cut into strips	1
1	celery stalk, thinly sliced	1
1	yellow pepper, thinly sliced	1
1	red pepper, thinly sliced	1
20	snow peas, ends trimmed	20
4	PASTENE Artichoke Hearts, quartered	4
1	PASTENE Hearts of Palm, sliced	1
1 tbsp	PASTENE Pesto Basil Sauce	15 mL
	PASTENE Linguine, cooked	
	salt and pepper	

- Heat oil in a skillet over medium-high heat. Add pork and stir-fry 4 minutes; season well. Remove meat and keep hot.
- Add vegetables to same skillet. Season with salt and pepper, and cook 3 minutes. Add pesto sauce and stir-fry 1 minute.
- Return meat to skillet and stir-fry 1 minute. Serve with hot cooked linguine.

TARRAGON VEAL MEDALLIONS
with Bocconcini

4 servings

¼ cup	PASTENE Pure Olive Oil	60 mL
1 lb	veal fillet sliced ½ inch (1 cm) thick	500 g
½ cup	dry white wine	125 mL
1 cup	veal or chicken stock	250 mL
4	balls of Bocconcini cheese, sliced	4
4 tbsp	pitted black olives, minced	60 mL
1 tbsp	chopped fresh tarragon salt and pepper	15 mL

- Preheat oven broiler.
- Heat olive oil in a skillet over medium-high heat. Add veal in several batches and sauté for 2 minutes on each side. Season well with salt and pepper and remove from skillet.
- Add wine to skillet and bring to boil. Add veal stock. Simmer for 5 minutes, and then set aside.
- Meanwhile, arrange veal on baking tray. Place bocconcini slices on top of veal, and garnish each slice with a dab of black olive spread. Sprinkle with chopped tarragon and place under broiler until cheese melts.
- Serve immediately with the wine sauce.

VEAL AND CAPER
Stew

4 servings

1½ lbs	cubed boneless veal	700 g
1 cup	all-purpose flour	250 mL
2 tbsp	PASTENE Pure Olive Oil	30 mL
2	garlic cloves, minced	2
1	red onion, finely chopped	1
½ tsp	dried oregano	2 mL
1 cup	dry white wine	250 mL
1 cup	PASTENE Diced Ready Spiced Tomatoes	250 mL
1 tbsp	chopped fresh basil	15 mL
¼ cup	PASTENE Capers in Vinegar, well drained	60 mL
1	envelope of demi-glace or brown gravy mix	1
	salt and pepper	

- Coat veal with flour. In an ovenproof skillet, heat olive oil over medium heat and cook veal for about 8 minutes, stirring occasionally, to brown on all sides. Add salt and pepper to taste.
- Add garlic, onion and oregano. Mix well and continue cooking for 5 minutes.
- Add wine and cook over medium-high heat for 4 minutes. Add tomatoes, and cook for 5 minutes at medium heat.
- Meanwhile, preheat oven to 350°F (180°C).
- Add basil and capers to veal mixture, then add demi-glace or gravy mix (dissolved according to package directions). Mix well and simmer for 5 minutes.
- Put skillet in oven and cook 1 hour. Serve with vegetables or rice.

VEAL MEDALLIONS
with Tomato Basil Sauce

4 servings

2½ tbsp	PASTENE Extra Virgin Olive Oil	40 mL
2	dry shallots, chopped	2
1	garlic clove, minced	1
1	can (28 fl. oz/796 mL) PASTENE Italian Peeled Tomatoes, drained and chopped	1
3 tbsp	PASTENE Pesto Basil Sauce	45 mL
1¼ lb	veal fillet, sliced 1 inch (2.5 cm) thick	600 g
½ cup	dry white wine	125 mL
	salt and pepper	
	PASTENE Fettucine	

- Heat 1 tbsp (15 mL) olive oil in a skillet over medium heat. Cook shallots and garlic 2 minutes. Stir in tomatoes and pesto sauce. Season to taste with salt and pepper; cook 15 minutes over high heat. Set aside.

- In another skillet, heat remaining oil and cook veal 2 minutes over medium heat. Turn veal, season to taste with salt and pepper; cook 1 minute. Remove from skillet and reserve.

- Cook wine in same skillet over medium-high heat. Stir in reserved tomato mixture and season to taste. Pour sauce over veal and serve immediately with hot, cooked fettucine.

Heat 1 tbsp (15 mL) olive oil in a skillet over medium heat. Cook shallots and garlic 2 minutes. Stir in tomatoes and pesto sauce.

In another skillet, heat oil and cook veal 2 minutes over medium heat. Turn veal, season to taste with salt and pepper; cook 1 minute. Remove from skillet.

Cook wine in same skillet over medium-high heat. Stir in reserved tomato mixture and season to taste.

VEAL CHOPS
Balsamico

4 servings

1 tbsp	PASTENE Pure Olive Oil	15 mL
4	veal chops, ¾ inch (2 cm) thick	4
¾ cup	PASTENE Balsamic Vinegar	175 mL
½ cup	white wine	125 mL
1 tbsp	chopped fresh thyme	15 mL
6	PASTENE Sundried Tomatoes in Oil, chopped	6
	salt and pepper	

- Preheat oven to 350°F (180°C).

- Heat oil in a large skillet until very hot. Season veal chops with salt and pepper. Sear quickly on both sides. Remove chops from skillet and place in baking pan in preheated oven. Bake until done to taste.

- Meanwhile, add vinegar to skillet. Stir over high heat about 5 minutes, scraping up and mixing with browned residue from bottom of pan.

- Add wine and cook another 5 minutes. Add thyme and sundried tomatoes. Lower heat and let simmer 2 minutes. Serve sauce over veal chops, accompanied with savoy cabbage, if desired.

CHICKEN
Cacciatore

6 servings

2 tbsp	PASTENE Pure Olive Oil	30 mL
12	chicken thighs	12
1	large onion, halved and sliced	2
2	garlic cloves, minced	2
1 cup	PASTENE "Kitchen Ready" Ground Tomatoes	250 mL
1	can (28 fl. oz/796 mL) PASTENE Diced Ready Spiced Tomatoes	1
½ cup	chicken stock	125 mL
⅔ cup	dry white wine	150 mL
1	sprig of fresh rosemary	1
1	bay leaf	1
1	jar (7 fl. oz/170 mL) PASTENE Roasted Peppers, drained and sliced	1
½ cup	PASTENE Pitted Olives	125 mL

- Preheat oven to 350°F (180°C).

- Heat olive oil in a large, ovenproof skillet. Add chicken and cook over medium heat until browned on both sides. Remove from skillet.

- In same skillet, cook onion and garlic about 5 minutes over medium heat. Stir in ground and diced tomatoes, chicken stock, wine, rosemary and bay leaf. Bring to a boil.

- Add reserved chicken and bake, uncovered, about 40 minutes or until chicken is tender. Stir in roasted peppers and olives, cook another 5 minutes, and serve immediately, with sauteed watercress if desired.

CHICKEN WITH SUNDRIED TOMATO
Stuffing

4-6 servings

1 cup	PASTENE Italian Arborio Rice, cooked al dente	250 mL
¼ cup	PASTENE Flavored Bread Crumbs	60 mL
⅓ cup	PASTENE Grated Parmesan Cheese	75 mL
8	PASTENE Sundried Tomatoes in Oil, drained and chopped	8
1 tbsp	chopped fresh oregano	15 mL
1 tbsp	PASTENE Pesto Basil Sauce	15 mL
1	egg	1
4	skinless, boneless chicken breast halves	4
2 tbsp	PASTENE Pure Olive Oil	30 mL
2	dry shallots, chopped	2
1 cup	chicken stock	250 mL
1 tbsp	PASTENE Balsamic Vinegar	15 mL
1 tbsp	cornstarch	15 mL
	salt and pepper	

- Preheat oven to 350°F (180°C).
- In a bowl, combine rice, bread crumbs, Parmesan, sundried tomatoes, oregano, pesto sauce and egg. Season with salt and pepper; set mixture aside.
- With a sharp knife, cut almost through chicken breasts lengthwise and open flat. Cover one half with rice and breadcrumb mixture; roll and tie closed with kitchen string.
- Heat olive oil in a skillet over medium-high heat. Cook chicken breasts until browned all over. Arrange chicken on a baking sheet and bake in oven 12-15 minutes, or until chicken is cooked through.
- Meanwhile, add shallots, chicken stock and vinegar to pan juices in skillet. Cook about 5 minutes. Dissolve the cornstarch in a little cold water and stir into skillet to thicken sauce. Serve sauce over slices of chicken with stuffing.

In a bowl, combine rice, bread crumbs, Parmesan, sundried tomatoes, oregano, pesto sauce and egg. Season with salt and pepper; set mixture aside.

With a sharp knife, cut almost through chicken breasts lengthwise and open flat.

Cover one half of chicken breasts with rice and breadcrumb mixture.

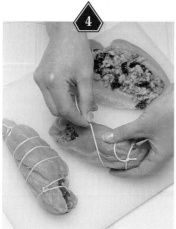

Roll each stuffed breast and tie closed with kitchen string.

Heat olive oil in a skillet over medium-high heat. Cook chicken breasts until browned all over. Remove chicken and place on a baking sheet.

Add shallots, chicken stock and vinegar to pan juices in skillet. Cook about 5 minutes. Dissolve the cornstarch in cold water and stir into skillet to thicken sauce.

167

NEW YORK STEAKS
with Mushroom Sauce

4 servings

3 tbsp	PASTENE Pure Olive Oil	45 mL
4	8 oz/225 g strip steaks or sirloin tips, fat trimmed	4
2	dry shallots, chopped	2
1	can (15 oz) PASTENE Broken Straw Mushrooms, drained and sliced, or ½ lb (250 g) sliced fresh mushrooms	1
2 cups	beef stock, heated	500 mL
2 tbsp	PASTENE Tomato Paste	30 mL
¼ cup	PASTENE "Kitchen Ready" Ground Tomatoes	60 mL
2 tbsp	35% cream	30 mL
1 tbsp	cornstarch	15 mL
3 tbsp	cold water	45 mL
1 tbsp	chopped fresh parsley salt and pepper	15 mL

- Heat 2 tbsp (30 mL) olive oil in large skillet over high heat. Add steaks and cook 2 minutes on each side or to taste. Remove steaks and keep warm.

- Add remaining oil to pan. Cook shallots and mushrooms 4 minutes over high heat; season well with salt and pepper.

- Mix in beef stock, tomato paste, and tomatoes; cook 3 minutes over medium heat. Stir in cream and cook 1 minute. Dilute cornstarch in the cold water; stir into sauce. Cook 2 minutes over medium heat, sprinkle with parsley and serve sauce with steaks.

ITALIAN-STYLE
Baked Chicken

4 servings

4	chicken legs	4
4 tbsp	PASTENE Extra Virgin Olive Oil	60 mL
1 tbsp	strong Dijon mustard	15 mL
2 cups	PASTENE Flavored Bread Crumbs	500 mL
1	jar (9 fl. oz/285 mL) PASTENE Italian Bruschetta	1
2 tbsp	PASTENE Balsamic Vinegar	30 mL
	salt and pepper	
	juice of 1 lemon	

- Preheat oven to 400°F (200°C).
- Skin chicken legs and season well with salt and pepper.
- In a bowl, mix olive oil, mustard and lemon juice. Dip chicken in this mixture to coat all sides, then roll in breadcrumbs.
- Place in single layer on baking pan and bake 40-45 minutes.
- Combine Bruschetta with Balsamic Vinegar and serve as dipping sauce with chicken.

LAMB KIDNEY
Sauté

4 servings

6	lamb kidneys	6
2-3 tbsp	all-purpose flour	30-45 mL
3 tbsp	PASTENE Pure Olive Oil	45 mL
1	green pepper, chopped	1
2	onions, chopped	2
1 tbsp	PASTENE Tomato Paste	15 mL
1 cup	chicken stock	250 mL
1	bay leaf	1
1 tbsp	fresh parsley, chopped	15 mL
	juice of 1 lemon	
	salt and pepper	

- Slice kidneys partly open lengthwise along outside curve. Remove visible fat. Cut kidneys into slices. Coat with flour.
- Heat olive oil in a heavy skillet over medium-high heat. Cook kidney slices lightly on both sides. Add green pepper and onions; cook at medium-low heat for 5 minutes.
- Add tomato paste, chicken stock, lemon juice, bay leaf, parsley, salt and pepper to taste. Cover tightly and cook 10-12 minutes, until kidneys are tender. Serve with rice and fresh asparagus.

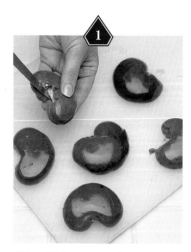

Slice kidneys partly open lengthwise along outside curve.

Remove visible fat. Cut kidneys into slices.

Coat kidney slices with flour.

Heat olive oil in a heavy skillet over medium-high heat. Cook kidney slices lightly on both sides.

Add green pepper and onions; cook at medium-low heat for 5 minutes.

Add tomato paste, chicken stock, lemon juice, bay leaf, parsley, salt and pepper to taste. Cover tightly and cook 10-12 minutes, until kidneys are tender.

RAINBOW TROUT
with Parmesan Tomato Stuffing

4-6 servings

2 tbsp	PASTENE Pure Olive Oil	30 mL
1	onion, finely chopped	1
1	garlic clove, minced	1
1	can (14 fl. oz/398 mL) PASTENE Italian Peeled Tomatoes, drained and chopped	1
1 cup	PASTENE "Kitchen Ready" Ground Tomatoes	250 mL
1 cup	cooked PASTENE Italian Arborio Rice	250 mL
¾ cup	PASTENE Grated Parmesan Cheese	175 mL
1 tbsp	chopped fresh parsley	15 mL
8	small rainbow trout fillets salt and pepper	8

- Heat half the olive oil in a medium skillet over medium-high heat. Add onion and cook about 5 minutes. Add garlic, chopped tomatoes, and ground tomatoes. Cook for 10 minutes.

- Preheat oven to 350°F (180°C).

- Remove pan from heat. Stir in rice, Parmesan, and parsley. Mix well and season to taste with salt and pepper. Set aside.

- Place one fillet skin-side down and cover with ¼ of the tomato-rice mixture. Cover with a second fillet, skin-side up. Press gently with your hand to remove air gaps.

- Arrange trout packages on an oiled baking dish. Bake 8-10 minutes, or until fish flakes easily when tested with a fork. Serve immediately.

VEAL
Parmigiana

4-6 servings

6	veal cutlets	6
¾ cup	all-purpose flour	175 mL
1	egg, lightly beaten	1
½ cup	low fat milk	125 mL
1⅔ cups	PASTENE Flavored Bread Crumbs	400 mL
8-10	fresh basil leaves	8-10
5 oz	Mozarella cheese, thinly sliced	150 g
	PASTENE Extra Virgin Olive Oil for frying	
	tomato sauce (see recipe on page 118)	

- Coat veal in flour, shaking off excess. Combine egg and milk. Dip veal slices in this mixture, then into breadcrumbs. Place in single layer on baking tray, cover, and refrigerate 10 minutes.

- Fry veal in hot olive oil over medium-high heat until browned and just cooked through; drain on absorbent paper.

- Place veal in single layer on baking tray, spoon tomato sauce over, and top with basil and cheese. Broil until cheese is melted. Serve with PASTENE pasta.

RASPBERRY
Chicken Breasts

4 servings

4	skinless, boneless chicken breasts halves	4
½ cup	PASTENE Extra Virgin Olive Oil	125 mL
4 tbsp	PASTENE Wine Vinegar	60 mL
2 cups	fresh raspberries	500 mL
2	dry shallots, chopped	2
1 cup	chicken stock	250 mL
½ cup	apple cider	125 mL
2	jars (6½ fl. oz/170 mL ea.) PASTENE Marinated Artichoke Hearts	2
	salt and pepper	
	PASTENE Pure Olive Oil for sautéing	

- Place chicken breasts in bowl and season with salt and pepper. Combine 6 tbsp (90 mL) olive oil, 2 tbsp (30 mL) vinegar and fresh raspberries (reserving a few to garnish the sauce); pour mixture over chicken. Marinate in refrigerator 1 hour.

- Preheat oven to 375°F (190°C).

- Heat remaining 2 tbsp (30 mL) olive oil in a skillet over medium-high heat. Add chicken (discarding marinade) and cook until browned on both sides. Remove from skillet to a baking pan, and bake 12 to 15 minutes, or until no longer pink inside.

- Meanwhile, add shallot to skillet. Cook 2 minutes. Stir in remaining vinegar, chicken stock, and apple cider. Let reduce slightly, then keep warm until chicken is cooked.

- In a second skillet, sauté the drained marinated artichokes in a little olive oil until heated through.

- Just before serving, stir reserved fresh raspberries into vinegar sauce. Simmer 2 minutes, then pour over chicken. Serve with warmed marinated artichokes.

MARINATED SALMON
with Olive Oil

4 servings

4	salmon fillets with skin, 5 oz (150 g) each	4
1 cup	PASTENE Extra Virgin Olive Oil	250 mL
1 tsp	chopped orange zest	5 mL
½ cup	fresh orange juice	125 mL
2 tbsp	PASTENE Wine Vinegar	30 mL
⅓ cup	sliced dry shallots	75 mL
2 tsp	chopped fresh tarragon	10 mL
½ tsp	black pepper	2 mL
	salt	

- Place salmon fillets in a large, shallow glass bowl.
- In a second bowl, combine olive oil, orange zest and juice, vinegar, shallots, tarragon, black pepper and salt to taste.
- Pour over salmon and let marinate at room temperature for ½ hour. Turn salmon and marinate another ½ hour.
- Preheat oven to broil.
- Place salmon, skin-side down, on oiled broiler pan. Baste with marinade and broil for 8 minutes, 3 inches (8 cm) from heat.
- To serve, spoon remaining marinade, heated for 3 minutes, over each serving. Fresh fennel and zucchini are good accompaniments.

SHRIMP AND OLIVE
Stir-fry

4 servings

2 tbsp	PASTENE Pure Olive Oil	30 mL
24	medium shrimps, peeled and deveined	24
1	green pepper, sliced	1
1	red pepper, sliced	1
1 tbsp	chopped fresh ginger	15 mL
1½ cups	PASTENE Italian Peeled Tomatoes, drained and chopped	375 mL
1 cup	chicken stock, heated	250 mL
2	PASTENE Hearts of Palm, sliced	2
⅓ cup	PASTENE Pitted Olives, sliced	75 mL
1 tsp	cornstarch	5 mL
2 tbsp	cold water	30 mL
	salt and pepper	

- Heat olive oil in skillet over medium heat. Add shrimps and cook 2 minutes. Turn shrimps over, season with salt and pepper and cook 1 minute. Remove from pan and set aside.
- In same skillet, stir-fry green and red peppers, and ginger for 2 minutes. Add chopped tomatoes and chicken stock. Cook 3 minutes.
- Add hearts of palm and olives.
- Dissolve the cornstarch in the cold water, then stir into tomato mixture. Cook until slightly thickened. Return shrimps to pan, season to taste with salt and pepper, and serve as soon as shrimps are heated through.

Salad Dressings
and
Marinades

There is a bewildering array of ready-
made salad dressings on the market,
but nothing tastes quite as good as one
that is fresh and homemade!

And there's nothing magical or
complicated about making your own
special dressing, vinaigrette or
marinade. All you need are top-quality
ingredients, such as Pastene's fine
selection of olive oils and vinegars,
and some simple, fresh flavorings.

To get you started, we've collected
some of our own favorite flavor
combinations. But when it comes
to salads and grilled foods, fresher is
better; so use herbs and spices that are
at their peak, and use your
imagination!

GORGONZOLA BALSAMIC VINAIGRETTE
with Pesto

makes about 1½ cups (375 mL)

1 cup	PASTENE Extra Virgin Olive Oil	250 mL
⅓ cup	PASTENE Balsamic Vinegar	75 mL
2 tbsp	PASTENE Pesto Basil Sauce	30 mL
2 tbsp	Gorgonzola or blue cheese	30 mL
	salt and freshly ground pepper	

- Combine first three ingredients until well mixed. Mash Gorgonzola with a fork, then stir into oil mixture. Season to taste with salt and pepper.

HERB
Vinaigrette

makes about 1½ cups (375 mL)

⅓ cup	PASTENE Wine Vinegar	75 mL
1 cup	PASTENE Extra Virgin Olive Oil	250 mL
1	garlic clove, minced	1
2 tsp	chopped fresh parsley	10 mL
2 tsp	chopped fresh basil	10 mL
2 tsp	chopped fresh thyme	10 mL
	salt and pepper	

- Combine all ingredients in a jar with a tight-fitting lid and shake vigorously. Refrigerate or serve immediately on salads or cooked vegetables.

ANCHOVY BALSAMIC
Vinaigrette

makes about 1½ cups (375 mL)

1 cup	PASTENE Extra Virgin Olive Oil	250 mL
⅓ cup	PASTENE Balsamic Vinegar	75 mL
4	PASTENE Anchovy Fillets in Olive Oil, drained and finely chopped	4
2	garlic cloves, minced	2
1 tbsp	finely chopped fresh parsley	15 mL
1 tbsp	finely chopped fresh thyme	15 mL
1 tbsp	finely chopped fresh oregano	15 mL
1	bay leaf	1

- Pour olive oil and balsamic vinegar in a jar with a tight-fitting lid. Shake well. Add remaining ingredients and shake vigorously until well mixed.
- This dressing is great with pasta salad, cold meats (especially pork), vegetables (such as PASTENE Roasted Peppers), greens, seafood, or grilled meats.

EXTRA VIRGIN OLIVE OIL AND ROASTED PEPPER
Vinaigrette

makes about 1½ cups (375 mL)

⅓ cup	PASTENE Roasted Peppers, drained and finely chopped	75 mL
1 cup	PASTENE Extra Virgin Olive Oil	250 mL
1 tbsp	finely chopped parsley	15 mL
1	garlic clove, minced	1
2 tbsp	PASTENE Balsamic Vinegar	30 mL
2 tbsp	PASTENE Wine Vinegar	30 mL
2	sprigs fresh thyme	2

• Combine all ingredients in a jar with a tight-fitting lid and shake vigorously. Serve on hot cooked vegetables or on salads.

ITALIAN TOMATO
Salad Dressing

makes about 2 cups (500 mL)

1	can (14 fl. oz/398 mL) PASTENE Italian Peeled Tomatoes	1
2 tbsp	PASTENE Wine Vinegar	30 mL
1	garlic clove, chopped	1
2 tbsp	Dijon mustard	30 mL
½ tsp	sugar	2 mL
¼ tsp	cracked black peppercorns	1 mL
¼ tsp	salt	1 mL
½ cup	PASTENE Extra Virgin Olive Oil	125 mL
	water	

• In a blender, combine tomatoes, vinegar, garlic, mustard, sugar, pepper, and salt until smooth. Add oil gradually in a thin stream with motor running.

• Stir in a little water if necessary to give desired consistency.

RED ONION
Dressing

makes about 1½ cups (375 mL)

1 cup	PASTENE Extra Virgin Olive Oil	250 mL
¼ cup	PASTENE Italian Wine Vinegar	60 mL
½ tsp	Dijon mustard	2 mL
1	red onion, finely chopped	1
½ tsp	dried oregano	2 mL
½ tsp	dried thyme	2 mL

• Combine all ingredients in a jar with a tight-fitting lid and shake vigorously until ingredients are well blended. Refrigerate for 1 hour before serving.

MAYONNAISE
Dressing

makes about 1¼ cups (300 mL)

1 tsp	Dijon mustard	5 mL
1	egg yolk	1
1 tbsp	fresh lemon juice	15 mL
1 cup	PASTENE Pure Olive Oil or Extra Virgin Olive Oil	250 mL
2 tbsp	PASTENE Wine Vinegar	30 mL
	pinch of cayenne	
	pinch of salt and pepper	

- Beat together mustard, egg yolk and lemon juice. Season with salt, pepper and cayenne.
- Add olive oil in a very thin stream, beating constantly with a rotary beater. Once all the oil has been added, beat in vinegar and continue beating until mixture is thick, adding more olive oil if necessary.

SPICY ITALIAN
Marinade

makes about 1 cup (250 mL)

⅓ cup	PASTENE Extra Virgin Olive Oil	75 mL
¼ cup	dry white wine	60 mL
2	garlic cloves, minced	2
1	red onion, finely chopped	1
1 tbsp	chopped fresh parsley	15 mL
1 tsp	dried oregano	5 mL
3	PASTENE Hot Finger Peppers, finely chopped	3
	salt and pepper	

- In a bowl, mix all ingredients with a fork.
- Use this marinade for any type of meat. (Meat should marinate at least 6 hours in refrigerator.)

BLACK OLIVE AND FENNEL
Marinade

makes about 2 cups (500 mL)

⅔ cup	PASTENE Extra Virgin Olive Oil	150 mL
½ cup	PASTENE Italian Wine Vinegar	125 mL
¼ cup	pitted black olives, minced	60 mL
¼ cup	finely chopped dry shallots	60 mL
½ cup	diced fennel bulb	125 mL
¼ tsp	fennel seeds	1 mL

- In a bowl, mix all ingredients with a fork.
- This marinade is especially good for dark meats such as beef, lamb, and Italian sausages.

WINE AND FRESH HERB
Marinade

makes about 1 cup (250 mL)

½ cup	PASTENE Extra Virgin Olive Oil	125 mL
¼ cup	PASTENE Wine Vinegar	60 mL
¼ cup	dry white wine	60 mL
1	bay leaf	1
1 tsp	chopped fresh thyme	5 mL
1 tsp	chopped fresh oregano	5 mL
2	garlic cloves, minced	2
8	peppercorns	8

- Mix olive oil, vinegar, and white wine with a fork.
- Add remaining ingredients and mix until well blended. Use this marinade for vegetables or chicken. (Marinate for at least 6 hours in refrigerator.)

GARLIC
Marinade

makes about 1 cup (250 mL)

2 tbsp	PASTENE Garlic Vinegar	30 mL
3	garlic cloves, minced	3
1 tbsp	Dijon mustard	15 mL
1 tbsp	chopped fresh parsley	15 mL
1 tsp	chopped fresh thyme	5 mL
¾ cup	PASTENE Extra Virgin Olive Oil	175 mL
¼ tsp	black pepper	1 mL

- In a bowl, mix vinegar, garlic, mustard, parsley, and thyme until well blended.
- In a second bowl, combine olive oil and black pepper. Whisk vinegar mixture into olive oil mixture. Use this marinade with fish, chicken or meat.

GREEN DRESSING
with Capers

makes about 2 cups (500 mL)

1 cup	PASTENE Extra Virgin Olive Oil	250 mL
2	egg yolks	2
¼ cup	PASTENE Wine Vinegar	60 mL
3 tbsp	PASTENE Capers in Vinegar, drained	45 mL
3 cups	fresh spinach, washed and drained	750 mL
	salt and pepper	

- In a blender or food processor, blend olive oil, egg yolks, and vinegar until smooth.
- Add capers and spinach and blend until well mixed. Season to taste with salt and pepper. This is a nice dressing for salads containing PASTENE Artichokes Hearts and PASTENE Hearts of Palm.

AÏOLI
Sauce

makes about 2½ cups (625 mL)

2 cups	PASTENE Extra Virgin Olive Oil	500 mL
3	egg yolks	3
6	garlic cloves, chopped	6
1	egg yolk	1
1 tsp	PASTENE Extra Virgin Olive Oil	5 mL
2 tbsp	PASTENE Garlic Vinegar	30 mL
2 tbsp	chopped fresh parsley	30 mL
	salt and pepper	
	fresh lemon juice	

- In a blender, combine first two ingredients to make a smooth mixture; pour into a bowl and set aside.
- In the same blender, combine garlic, 1 egg yolk, 1 tsp (5 mL) olive oil, vinegar, and parsley until smooth and creamy.
- Add garlic mixture to the first mixture. Season with salt and pepper and lemon juice to taste. This classic sauce is delicious with cold steamed vegetables, salads or fish.

SUNDRIED TOMATO
Pesto

makes about 1 cup (250 mL)

12	PASTENE Sundried Tomatoes in Oil, drained	12
½ cup	PASTENE Extra Virgin Olive Oil	125 mL
2 tbsp	PASTENE Wine Vinegar	30 mL
1 tbsp	garlic, minced	15 mL
½ cup	PASTENE Grated Parmesan Cheese	125 mL
	salt and pepper	

• Place in blender the tomatoes, olive oil, vinegar, basil, and garlic. Process until smooth. Add salt and pepper to taste.

• Add Parmesan and process until combined. This is delicious on pasta, or as a topping for crostini.

ESSENTIAL
Vinaigrette

makes about 1½ cups (375 mL)

⅓ cup	PASTENE Wine Vinegar	75 mL
2 tsp	Dijon mustard	10 mL
¼ tsp	salt	1 mL
¼ tsp	chopped fresh parsley	1 mL
¼ tsp	black pepper	1 mL
1 cup	PASTENE Extra Virgin Olive Oil	250 mL

• Combine vinegar, mustard, salt, parsley and pepper in a jar with a tight-fitting lid and shake vigorously.

• Slowly add olive oil in a thin stream, stirring constantly and vigorously with a fork.

BLACK OLIVE
Vinaigrette

makes about 1¼ cups (300 mL)

½ cup	PASTENE Extra Virgin Olive Oil	125 mL
½ cup	PASTENE Garlic Vinegar	125 mL
20	PASTENE Pitted Black Olives	20
2	garlic cloves, minced	2
1 tbsp	finely chopped fresh parsley	15 mL
1 tbsp	finely chopped fresh thyme	15 mL
1 tbsp	finely chopped fresh oregano	15 mL
1	bay leaf	1

• Combine all ingredients in a blender until smooth. Serve with greens or pasta salads.